Be The Ultimate Sports Coach

The Definitive Practical Guide to Coaching
Youth Sports. The How, The Why,
and What to Avoid

By Allen D. Buck

"Then why don't they coach that way?"

That was the answer I received when, after completing this book, I ran into Don, a person I had coached against a dozen years prior. I told him about the book, not to promote it but because he is in the book. I told him that it is directed at helping coaches develop the right attitude toward how to best help their players and that experienced or inexperienced coaches would not disagree with anything I wrote. He interrupted me to say, "Then why don't they coach that way!?!"

Exactly! That is my whole point in writing this book. Thank you, Don, for giving me the validation that there is a need for the lessons in this book.

TABLE OF CONTENTS

PREFACE

I am the product of educators. My father was a high school principal and my mother was a stay-at-home mom prior to teaching math, English, and whatever else was needed for adults to attain their GEDs. Education was important in our family and I was raised with a strong sense of right vs. wrong. My coaches were firm taskmasters so I was no stranger to hard work in all aspects of life. The principles I learned from my parents and coaches serve as the basis for my approach to coaching.

I have two adult sons. When they were three and seven, their mother and I divorced. She moved several states away so I gained custody and raised my sons. I recognized very early that these were not quiet, mild-mannered children. Since I knew sports, I channeled their ample energies into athletics. Naturally I followed. That was the beginning of my love affair with coaching.

I have coached football, basketball, and baseball for over twenty-five years. My players have ranged in age from 6 to 18 year old seniors in high school. There are certain coaching skills that are needed more at one level than at others, but the basic principles remain the same throughout this age range. I also provide radio commentary in football, basketball, baseball, and softball. I have done play-by-play but my specialty is analysis and color. Game knowledge and the ability to communicate it serve me very well in both, coaching and broadcasting.

I was fortunate to have a good upbringing and a strong education. I was lucky to have coaches whose messages went beyond the sport and dovetailed nicely with the principles I learned at home. I have passed these principles along to many players over the years but I have seen too many coaches who did not grasp this concept. It is my hope that this book will help coaches everywhere to understand that the best coaching involves more than just the "X"s and "O"s.

INTRODUCTION

I wrote this book for every child who ever participates in team sports. I firmly believe that every coach's top priority when coaching should be the betterment of the kids he coaches. The information in this book will help coaches better help their players, and when that happens, the book will have served its purpose. I do not address college or professional coaching because that is an entirely different bailiwick.

Coaching can be one of the most rewarding things you'll ever do. Coaching can be one of the most frustrating things you'll ever do. When it's all said and done, which statement is true is largely up to you. Can I promise you success if you read my book? No. But, whether you are a brand new coach or one with experience who wants to improve; this book is a good place to start.

*****Since I have sons and have only coached boys so far, I have written this book with reference to the male gender. Please do not be offended if you are a lady or if you have daughters. There is no gender slight intended; it is just easier to write without saying, "him/her," etc. throughout the book and maybe I'm not smart enough to keep everything straight that way anyhow. *****

While I'm on the subject, let me say that one of the best coaches I ever watched work is a lady who coached the girls' basketball teams at the high school where I coached. Her knowledge of the sport was superior; her passion for coaching was second to none; and her ability to inspire her players to the best of their potential - on and off the court - was incredible. Isn't that what all coaches should strive to be? I am proud to say that I learned a lot from her.

Like many coaches, I got involved when my sons were just starting to play competitive athletics. I was not impressed with what I

1

saw in their first coaches so I got involved. I don't mean to sound arrogant, but too many coaches are in it to make stars out of their own children and their buddies' kids, etc. Sadly, much of this remains the same even among high school coaches. That is the basis for one of the wrong reasons to coach. (What to avoid.)

I approached the whole world of youth athletics differently than other coaches I had watched and I'm glad I did. My style is basically coaching from the kids up; not from the coach down. When I got to the high school level, I found that the same principles I used in youth sports applied to those ages too. What I learned along the way is priceless. In this book, I will share the secrets that I learned; some as a result of successful techniques I had worked to develop and others that I happened upon by accident.

I have been asked about my coaching record. I must admit that I have no idea what it is. That's probably because I had a job as a salesman so coaching was not my profession. I never focused on my record; I focused on the kids. I have put together over sixty teams in football, basketball, and baseball and, although I don't know my record in any sport, I do know that every few years, my teams won championships. Along the way, there was a number of undefeated seasons so, by the usual standards, I have been successful. But building my resume is not why I coach and my record as a coach is not how I define my success. I coach for the betterment of the kids - and their success is far more important than my record.

I did not write this book as an, "ABCs," directive to coaching because I don't think such a book can be written. You see, coaching is like marriage or raising children in that there can't be *one perfect instruction manual*. Think of this book as a cookbook of sorts. You will find many techniques (recipes) that you will follow to the letter. You will find others that you will utilize and modify to fit your specific situation.

Still other techniques will spawn new ideas that will help you in your quest to be a better coach.

While I believe very firmly that some of the things I stress are absolutely correct in the coaching arena, I realize that everyone's coaching situation is different. For anyone to be adamant about exactly how to handle every aspect of coaching would be terribly naïve and shortsighted; hence, *there is no such thing as a perfect coaching instructional manual.*

What you will read is a series of vignettes describing various coaching situations I have encountered and how I handled them. In some cases, I relate situations that I have watched other coaches deal with; some good and some not so good. In those instances, I help you to see options that will get the best results out of the players. (That's the goal, isn't it?)

You will see that I follow the same set of principles in all that I do. From that, you will determine what I deem to be the most important aspects of competitive athletics and why. While I take the responsibility of coaching very seriously – you probably have not met a more competitive person than I – I do not take myself too seriously. Much of what you read will have my offbeat sense of humor injected into it. Hopefully, that will make this an easy read while still being helpful as you prepare to embark, or continue, on your coaching journey.

If you finish this book and your answers to the questions it is intended to provoke are not what they should be, then you may not be cut out for coaching. Do yourself, and every child you might potentially impact, a favor by collecting stamps, gardening, or fishing...anything but coaching! If you still feel you're up to the challenge – for all of the right reasons – go for it!

*Footnote: While I believe you will find this book to be very easy and entertaining to read, I promise the second chapter will be a bit more tedious than the rest. Don't get me wrong; it won't be pure torture and you do need to get through it any way you can because it is an extremely important chapter. It lays the groundwork for everything else that follows. (Hey, at least you're getting fair warning.) But rest assured, the remainder of the book will be more entertaining to read as you explore some of the solutions to issues you will encounter in your efforts toward becoming the best coach you can be.

Be The
Ultimate
Sports Coach

I. Why do you want to be a coach?

NOTE: If you have not read the Introduction, I recommend that you do so. The information in it is integral to understanding the basis for how and why this book is structured the way that it is. Because that information is so critical to the entire book, I almost used it as a first chapter. Anyway, if you take a few minutes to go back and read the Introduction first, I think you'll be glad you did. Thank you.

Before you even make that first phone call or approach that first league official about becoming a coach, ask yourself why. Believe me, no matter what your answer to this first question is, if you decide to get involved coaching kids, you'll be asking yourself that same question over and over until it's over. (Why? *Why? !*#@&% WHY!?!*) Just kidding here. Coaching and being involved with kids of all ages is a lot of fun. Frustrating at times, but nevertheless fun overall.

There are all sorts of reasons why people get involved coaching youth sports. Maybe their wives encourage them as a way of coaxing uninvolved dads to spend more time with their sons. Maybe they are afraid little Johnny won't get to play unless Dad is the coach. Maybe they

1

can see that multi-million dollar payoff at the signing of the big professional contract. Some erstwhile coaches are frustrated former athletes who still have some unresolved issues from their youth. We've all seen these types of coaches and hopefully; reading this book will inspire you to be better than these examples.

Anyway, all of those are the wrong reasons to get involved in coaching. There is only one reason to coach and that is for the benefit of the kids. If you are doing it for any other reason, get out. I am very adamant about this. The kids deserve the best of everything you've got to offer. If the kids' benefits are not your top priority, you are being unfair to the athlete. Get out. Get out now. Do not pass go. Do not collect $200.

You really have to *want* to coach to become a youth coach. You see, when you're the coach, you don't get any down time. You don't have any choices, i.e., do I stay home and watch the big game on TV or do I go to practice? No decision here. You go to practice. Do I stop for a beer with the boys on the way home from work or do I go to practice? You go to practice. Do I plan a golf game or a fishing trip for Saturday? No. You go to practice. *Always!* You don't even mow your lawn when you want because it might interfere with practice. It's kind of like being married; you're no longer the boss of your own schedule. (Hey, just kidding on that last point.) There's my witty(?) sense of humor.

Life, as you know it, changes when you become the coach. Your time is no longer yours to do with as you please. You are at the mercy of the schedule as dictated by the league. The point is that you will be making many sacrifices for the success of your program and you will get much more enjoyment doing all that is necessary if you are coaching for the right reason. If not, many of those tasks will become burdensome; you will begin to resent – instead of enjoy - much of what you're doing; and this will result in you not giving your very best to the kids.

Part of this coaching deal is being the leader and that usually means leading by example. You will be held to a higher standard. Remember, many of the kids you're going to be involved with don't have Ozzie and Harriet at home to teach them responsibility. (Ozzie and Who?) That's a big part of the coach's job. Everything you do is, in some small way, helping teach your players - and their parents - about responsibility to the team and to the individual himself.

Players aren't expected to show up late; coaches are expected to show up early…*really* early. (Remember the higher standard.) If one kid gets to the park even moments before you do, you're late. It doesn't matter how early you are. That kid could be thirty minutes early for practice, but if you're not there waiting on his undoubtedly smiling face, then you're late. If you're not the first one there, in some small way, you have failed that player and that parent. Your program now has a chink in its armor. We can't let that happen needlessly for there will be plenty of times when there will be a real, actual honest-to-goodness chink in your armor, not just the imagined kind.

3

As a coach, you use the DVR a lot. You read the paper when all you can see is the inside of your own eyelids. Meals come…well, you order from the clown's mouth quite often. You begin to think of the ballparks that have the grill going full bore during games as your own personal five star restaurants. Popcorn is a popular side dish. Vegetables? I always considered Mountain Dew to be a vegetable. It's green, isn't it? Close enough.

I got involved after the first year my boys played baseball. During that first season, I watched how the coaches handled the players. I observed what the coaches could offer the players in terms of the knowledge of baseball; the skills they could teach; and what they could add to the value of the whole team sport experience. What I saw is why I got involved.

Now, first, let me say that of the sports I've coached, baseball is by far my weakest sport as far as knowledge of the game. The coaches I saw were not horrible people, - not axe murderers or anything like that. They just didn't have a good grasp of the sport; a good handle on how to run a team; or how to relate to the kids. So I stepped up to the plate. (Clever play on words, eh?)

Also, as I sat in the stands watching *all* of their practices and *all* of their games that first year, I figured: I'm here already so, "Why not?" Also, it occurred to me that since I was going to be at each event anyway, what better way to get out of working the concession stand than to be the coach? *I'm kidding here.*

O. k., so dodging concession stand duty is a lousy reason to coach and, as a single dad, it would remove me from a golden opportunity to rub elbows with all of the good-looking moms. No, not really. Actually, as tempting as it may seem, I had a hard and fast rule to never get involved with any players' moms. I wanted to be sure I remained totally objective and true to my mantra that the best benefit of each kid was the most important reason for coaching…but I digress. Now back to the *wrong* reasons to coach.

As previously mentioned, another reason people choose to coach is to protect their children. Maybe you are afraid Little Johnny won't get to play unless Dad is the coach. Your heart may be in the right place, but this motivation has disaster written all over it. First, let me assure you that the kids on the team know at a very early age who the better players are. Oh, sure, you get some kids who try to bully their way to the front of the line. (That never changes; as I've gotten older, I still see that sort of behavior from people rumored to be grown-ups.) Generally, by the time the kids are in the 7 – 8 year old range, they know who the better players are and what their strengths and weaknesses are. Who the better players are will change as the years go by and puberty takes over so if you're ranking players now, do it in pencil not pen; carry a big eraser; and don't be afraid to use it.

Maybe, as seems to be the case all too often, you can see that multi-million dollar payoff at the signing of Little Johnny's big professional contract. Far too many dads get that idea in their heads that Little Johnny is the next great athlete of the modern era. There are so many things wrong with that presumption; I'm not going to get into it here. I'm sure many psychologists have written entire books covering just that one topic. Heck, there's probably an entire section in the library devoted solely to books dealing with this phenomenon. (Is this really a "phenomenon"? Maybe it's just a tendency...)

Basically, it's simple; encourage your kid to do what he enjoys and let him know you're there to lend any support he wants. But don't push! It might make him push back. Think about your wife's last home improvement project. How long did it take for you to complete the task that was the top priority on your wife's 'Honey Do' list? *(I'll get it done; you don't have to remind me every six months.)*

Remember, you want this to be a fun time in your child's life. (O. k., secretly you still *want* him to be the next big superstar.) The best way for it to be enjoyable to him is if he is at least somewhat good at it. The best way for that to happen is for him to want to practice. The best way to make him want to practice is by letting it be his idea.

The two most motivated kids I ever had the pleasure of coaching were the sons of a high school baseball coach. I know what you're thinking. *'Oh, no; not another case where these poor kids had to play dad's sport or they never would have gotten his attention.'* Wrong! Quite the opposite actually. This was an exception to the norm and a great family situation. (Had you fooled there for a moment, didn't I?)

I met the dad while coaching 7 – 8 year old pitching machine baseball. He helped our district Pony League teams before his high school practices started in earnest in the spring. He told me he never asked his sons to play catch, hit balls, or shag flies, but if they ever asked him, he never – ever - refused. Understand; he could have just walked in the door from a full day of teaching school and several hours of a rigorous high school practice. It didn't matter. No matter how tired he was, he never said no.

Think about that approach. First of all, when a kid is eager to do something, he will be much more willing to give his best effort. He can be working his tail off and be happy about it because he is doing what he enjoys. Secondly, the kid gets positive reinforcement from the dad who will, at all costs, go out and play ball. (Again, the psychologists have covered this topic ad nauseam.)

I can see some very motivated dads having a hard time with this. I can be rather driven and not very patient, but thankfully my sons always wanted to practice football, basketball, or baseball – whatever was in season. (Our seasons lasted twelve months per year for each sport.) This example, set by an extremely successful high school coach, is one I would suggest keeping in your tool bag.

Remember the important thing here. It was always the kids' idea to go out and play ball. They took ownership of their own progress and fortunately, they had the best tools around to help them. Their dad was the best baseball coach I've ever been around and their grandfather was also a veritable font of baseball knowledge. I learned much of my technical knowledge and a lot about patience from these two gentlemen. It is important to note here that this coach won two state high school baseball championships in a three-year period, a couple more since then, and he's not done yet. His sons went to college on baseball scholarships and one is coaching college baseball. Pretty good results using his approach, eh?

Another brief lesson; keep your eyes and ears open and if you find a resource like these guys from whom you can learn, use them for all they're worth. Remember, you're trying to be the best coach you can be for the sake of your young players. It doesn't matter where the knowledge comes from as long as it helps the kids.

That's the main message here; help the kids. Your record as coach is totally irrelevant. (Remember, I don't even know mine!) Now before you throw this book away, please understand, I am not talking about *not keeping score.* I mean; that would just be stupid. Our focus is on teaching the kids to be competitive so that it helps them in their future endeavors, both on and off the field, court, or wherever they play. Keeping score is an extremely important part of that. Your goal always is to win but you're going to be teaching a lot more than just the rules of the game and those other things are more important than your record anyway.

* * * * * *

Have you ever seen the peewee basketball team with the one kid who can dribble the ball down the floor faster than anybody else on the other team? Quite often, you will see that coach - *and I'm using that term very loosely here* - structure his team so that this player runs amok. Kids that age will do plenty of amok running without the help and encouragement of his youth league basketball coach. With that one player being the only kid on the court doing anything remotely resembling basketball, and the other players running around trying to look helpful while making sure they don't actually get involved in the action, the only kid gaining any benefit is that one little whirling dervish.

His team will win lots of games. His coach will win lots of games – evidence of how good the coach is, right? Meanwhile, you have eight other kids who have been told that they've had fun because their team won. They haven't learned anything: they're no better after the season than they were before the season. What's more, the little buzz saw dribbling machine really hasn't learned anything either.

You can always spot this kid when he gets a little older and players start to broaden their game to actually include things such as passing. As good as this junior phenom was, (remember all those games his team won in pee-wee leagues?), he never developed those other skills he'd need to be able to play in high school. Thanks, youth league coach. (…Who was so insecure he made sure his teams won all the games regardless of the fact that his players learned nothing!) We've all seen coaches like that so it won't be hard to avoid that approach with your teams.

******

I was privileged to watch the antithesis of this type of coach one basketball season. One of the coaches in our league was a very smart individual with a very bright basketball mind. I knew his players would be lucky to have him as a coach but I was not prepared for the "Wow" factor that I would encounter watching his team progress throughout the season.

This coach was unable to attend the coaches' meeting when the teams were chosen. He entrusted the rest of the coaches to be fair in selecting his team for him. (Silly man.) Just kidding. Actually, we were absolutely fair with him and it started out very badly for the rest of the league.

In this league, we had an evening of player evaluations where the players went through some skill stations. The coaches made notes concerning such things as height, ball handling ability, speed, walking and chewing gum, etc. At the selection meeting, the coaches determined that the league would have eight teams. We then divided the players into groups according to skill level with eight players in each group.

This system will work only if the coaches evaluate players honestly and do not "hide" any players for later use. I have seen a coach tell a very good player not to sign up until after teams were chosen so he can finagle the kid onto his team. Most leagues will allow late sign-ups and they will have a way of allocating those players to teams. A devious coach can figure out the system and rig things so when this really good player signs up late, that coach will get him on his team. (Please avoid that!)

We were fortunate that year in this regard. The coaches were honest. Also, the coaches had a lot of experience and familiarity with the players so it was relatively easy to group the players according to skills, height, etc. We then put the names of the first eight players in a hat and had a blind draw. We did reserve the right for a coach to bring up any matters that might make it uncomfortable for a player to be on his team. For example, maybe a player and the coach's son don't get along or maybe the parents don't get along. In cases like that, we put the player's name back in the hat or agreed on a suitable trade. We didn't want to create any problems before the season even started.

The other exception to the blind draw concerned coaches' kids. When it was time to draw a group with a coach's kid in it, the coach was given his kid automatically. To prevent coaches from stacking teams, we did not allow coaches to pick their assistants prior to the draw. That prevented the two dads with the best two players in the league from joining forces before the draw even took place.

We began the draw with the biggest (and often best) players. When we drew for the absentee coach, sure enough, he got the best player in the league. This kid was always bigger and more athletic than his classmates. He was also very intelligent and an all around good egg. (He went on to play Big Ten football so yes, he was a *terrific* athlete.) After that one selection, this coach's luck ran out. In each of the remaining seven groups, his draw was the worst player. The draw was not rigged; it just happened that way.

This coach didn't bat an eye. He never questioned the fairness of the draw. He simply taught his team how to play basketball. He could have had the all-star do everything and just have the other players stay out of the way. He didn't. When other teams pressed, his players ran specific plays and worked the ball around to break the press. They could have thrown the ball up high to their big guy and let him bring the ball up as other players bounced off of him or ran and hid from him.

This team didn't do that. This coach taught these kids how to rely on themselves and all of their teammates. They developed skills far better than they would have if they had been on another coach's team. This is the kind of coach you want to be, - especially in youth sports. What a fantastic approach and an inspiration to other coaches. WOW!

When you coach at higher levels, you have the ability to cut players but even after keeping only the players you want, you still might encounter weaknesses in your team. You had better deal with them early and develop the skills in those weaker players so when you need their contributions later in the season, they will be able to deliver. Maybe the extent of their contributions is nothing more than playing hamburger against the starters. Still, the better they are, the harder they can push your studs and ultimately the better they help make your team. Learning the importance of working with and developing your lesser skilled players will make you a better coach and will improve your teams.

* * * * * *

Let's look at another reason not to coach. Have you ever noticed that some erstwhile coaches are frustrated former athletes who still have some unresolved issues from their youth? You can spot these coaches a mile away and they are rarely good influences on the players they coach.

If you have looked at your personal situation, and can honestly say that you can approach the team with a completely altruistic attitude, then you have an outside chance at being successful, (which we will define shortly), and your players will have an opportunity to have an enjoyable season. That's why you're here.

Face it, when you become the coach, it isn't about you; it's about your players. That has to be your focus if you really want to succeed. Don't think you can fake it; your players will know if you're sincere or not.

Take the following example from a local high school football coach. After watching a rather disappointing performance by a high school football team, I ran into one of the seniors on the team. The first half was good, but the second half was anything but. I asked this player what his football coach had said at halftime of the game. What he told me was very disheartening.

First, let me tell you about this player. He was a coach's dream. He was very enthusiastic and always worked very hard. During wind sprints, this undersized lineman competed with the backs to get faster. When he was a sophomore, he picked the toughest player on the varsity to go up against during hitting drills. He got the snot kicked out of himself, but he knew that competing with the best was the quickest way to get better. Weighing only 175 pounds, he was in the 1000+ pound club. That 'club' is for players who could lift a total of 1000 pounds combined in three lifts: bench press, squat, and dead lift. Normally, this club is exclusive to linemen weighing well over 200 pounds, yet this 'skinny, little' kid made it. You get the picture.

The team had lost a game in which they were very competitive in the first half. This team's record was not very good that year so being competitive in the first half was a really good start. In the second half, the players came out flat. They had no spring in their step. Their play was lackluster and, of course, they lost.

After such an encouraging first half of inspired play, it was disappointing to see the lack of determination in the second half. I was curious what went on at halftime to produce such a lethargic second half performance. Without pointing out the obvious to this player, I asked him what the coaches told them at the half.

I could tell he was very discouraged when he said, in a very matter-of-fact manner, that the assistant coach did most of the talking. He told me the coach ranted, raved, and yelled at them to try to pump them up, but it was so artificial that he quit listening. It must have been bad if this coach's halftime speech took this kid with his great attitude and turned him off, leaving him dejected when he came out to play a second half of football. If this coach had that much of a negative effect on this player with the gung-ho attitude, just think what effect he had on the other players.

We've all seen games in which a trailing team comes tearing out of the locker room ready to rip into the opposing team. Heck, the players might've ripped the locker room door off of its hinges to get to the start of the second half. Something got into that team in the locker room to make its collective members so determined to win the game that they would not be denied. Do you think this pride and determination to succeed surfaced just because they got yelled at during halftime? I don't think so.

Why do you think some coaches can get that type of inspired performance out of their teams and others can't? It isn't just the yelling. One of the biggest factors is the coach's belief in his players. The successful coach knows what his players are capable of and believes in their ability to reach that potential. He knows how to push the right buttons to get the very best out of his players. And yes, he might yell at them from time to time, but it is never to denigrate and humiliate them. It is to inspire them to the greatness that lies within each player.

Now, think about the high school coach in this example. Do you think this coach is there for the kids or is he there for some other reason, like maybe his resume? I don't know the answer to that question, but I do know this: if you don't believe what you're preaching, the players won't believe it either. You can't fake it. Your players will see right through you. I think you can see that this is another example of *what to avoid!*

* * * * * *

At one point, I was coaching a 6th grade All-Star basketball team. We travelled to weekend tournaments after the school seasons were finished. There is a lot of valuable experience the kids can get from these events. Obviously these tournaments provide tougher competition and we all know the best way to get better is to play tougher competition.

The players gain exposure to kids from other areas that may have totally different styles of play. Quite frankly, sometimes the difference between one player and another is the number of games they play. One kid can play on his school team only and play ten games in a year. Another kid can play on his school team, feeder league, tournament travel team, and a summer league and play seventy-five games in a year. Given equal talent, it seems fairly obvious that when one player plays a significant mount more than the other, he will develop his talent more completely. Not only that, the experiences of the travel, meeting players from other areas, and maybe getting to spend some one-on-one time with a parent who travels with the kid are all good benefits too.

While some of the league coaches were discussing details about this all-star team, the players, and how to best prepare them for future success, the older brother of one of the league players spoke up. He just happened to be a coach at the high school that most of these kids would attend. His comment was, "We already know who the basketball players are going to be at 'XYZ' High School anyway." He basically dismissed these additional tournaments as an exercise in futility because, as one of the people in control of these boys' athletic future, he had already made up his mind.

We were all so stunned we didn't know what to say. His comment was utterly absurd on many levels. Plus, since he was on the, "inside," anything we would have said might have jeopardized our kids' future opportunities. The bizarre nature of that statement is more typical of the prevailing attitudes of high school coaches than you would ever imagine. There are too many variables involved in the development of players so if you want to maintain a successful program, you'd better keep all options open. This coach was (and still is) clueless as to what it takes to be a good high school coach. This kind of attitude is definitely one to avoid.

At this age, 11 – 13, the boys have barely hit puberty yet so who's to say how any of the boys are going to develop physically in the next few years? Not only that, there are many other options and interests that might draw a young man's attention as he matriculates through adolescence.

Kids can choose any one of many sports offered in schools these days. There are other school activities such as the band, theater, speech and debate, and so many extracurricular school sponsored activities that can take a kid out of the specific sport that you penciled him in at age eleven. I have not even mentioned Susie from chemistry class who might become a formidable competitor for a young man's attention.

If you haven't figured it out yet, I am incredulous at the arrogance and ignorance of this coach's statement. To anoint certain kids several years ahead of time at the exclusion of the others is, to put it kindly, shortsighted. The better way to handle teams at this age is to work with and develop as many players as possible so you can build a broad base for your high school program. You should know going in that you will lose many players over the years due to attrition. More on that later.

* * * * * *

One of the more prevalent reasons that coaches coach is for their resumes. Their goal is to put up a nice record in the short term and then move to a better opportunity. Don't get me wrong; I am not faulting a career coach for trying to better himself. In any career, that should be the goal. But remember, you are working with kids. I've seen many coaches build their resumes without regard to their players, quickly move on, and leave a lot of damaged kids in their wake. This isn't necessary. There are better ways to proceed and good coaches are cognizant of the impact they have on their players and programs. Remember, you're the grown up and those kids don't deserve to end up on the bottom of your shoe.

I once had this very discussion with a high school football coach. He coached in my area for seven seasons and after four of those, he applied for other jobs at, "more prestigious," schools in other areas. Just how committed do you think that coach was to developing the program at that school and working with those kids?

Although he won many football games while he was there, he did not field the best team he had during any of his first six years because he always had a hidden agenda. That means he left better players on the bench and in his wake. Why? I'm glad you asked; that shows that you're paying attention. There are many answers to that question, so bear with me as you learn some things to avoid.

This coach actually epitomizes several of the absolute worst reasons to coach. (Remember, that's what we're trying to avoid.) He left his former school at the end of his son's freshman year. His son was a quarterback and there was another quarterback the same age competing for the position. This other player would eventually earn a college scholarship and a spot on an NFL roster. Can you say talent? This kid had it and obviously, the coach's son would never be the star quarterback with this very talented athlete on the team.

The coach left that school to find one where his son could be the starting quarterback. (We've already touched on fathers who coach for their sons' playing time.) When this coach came to the school in my area, there was a quarterback the same age as his son who had started a few games during his freshman year. This player was a very gifted quarterback. The coach used a minor summertime disciplinary infraction to suspend the kid for three games at the beginning of his sophomore season. The coach inserted his son as the starting quarterback during the other player's suspension. Granted, the son knew dear old dad's offense, but he also brought along a very mediocre arm (I'm being kind here) and all of the speed of the Statue of Liberty. (O.K., not so kind there.) They ran a triple option offense so speed was a huge asset at the quarterback position.

Up to this point, I still wouldn't fault the coach, because after all, discipline is one of the most important lessons you can teach as a coach. The starter made a mistake and he needed to accept his punishment. The coach starting his son in replacement duty was an acceptable stopgap measure. But what the coach did next is inappropriate at any level of coaching.

As with many programs, the team's schedule had several cupcakes to start the season. Because of this, the Band-Aid QB was successful. That's when the coach told the star-in-the-making that he wouldn't get his position back when his suspension was over because the offense was, "clicking," and he didn't want to disrupt it. "Clicking?" Heavens, the JV team could have won those games against the weakest teams on the schedule.

Any time a coach has a son on his team, it can create a very tenuous situation. The coach and the player need to talk about that long before the situation arises. If they can't come to an appropriate understanding for the good of everyone, they shouldn't enter into the player and coach relationship. Regardless of anything else, if the coach has a son on the team, there must be no special treatment.

Anyway, the stud quarterback, to his credit, played out the season at safety but he never took another snap - not even during mop-up time during any of the many blowouts. After all, the coach wouldn't want the legions of fans to see just how good this kid was; they might start asking questions. During the summer, the young man asked the coach if he could compete for the position. The coach told him no. He wanted to stay with his son at QB. This star athlete eventually quit the team, focused solely on basketball, and wound up earning a Division I basketball scholarship.

This young man handled his adversity exceptionally well, but the point is; he should not have been put in that situation at all. A coach should have the best interests of all of the players and the team at the top of his priorities – without regard to his son (or any other specific player). The irony here is that if the coach works to bring each player to the best of his potential and do the same with the team as a whole, ultimately the team will provide the coach with a better resume than if the coach focused on the resume from the start. I call that, "Coaching from the players up, not from the coach down."

This coach wasn't done. He continued coaching for his resume, not the players. (…while sending plenty of those resumes to prospective employers after each season.) For the next four seasons, he coddled a very talented class with the goal of winning a state championship – regardless of how many other players' careers he sacrificed along the way. As a coach, you always want to win the ultimate prize and in this case it was a state championship. I understand that and I agree with it fully.

The point is; he could have accomplished that by playing the best players every year, not just the best players from one class at the expense of all others. As the coach, you're supposed to be teaching how to compete. Part of competing is winning your position or losing your position based on your ability and performance. Players expect that and they can live with the disappointment of getting beaten out for a position – as long as it is fair competition.

I once told this coach that he could coach there as long as he liked, but the players only had four years. The only thing they had to hold onto was the idea that if they gave their best effort and proved they were the best at their positions, they would play. Coaches should not choose players; the competition among the players should do that. It is unfair to take that opportunity to compete away from a kid. I looked him right in the eye when I made that point, but I could see that he did not understand. He just didn't get it. (You know; the lights were on but nobody was home.) *Kids deserve the opportunity to compete for their positions.* Period.

A parent once struck up a conversation with this coach in the spring of the year. They discussed football in general and the prospects for the team the next season. The father brought up the subject of his son, who would be a senior in the fall - one year ahead of the very talented class with which you are familiar. He was the best quarterback on the team. The players knew it; opposing coaches knew it; and anyone who was at all familiar with this team and the game of football knew it.

The man told the coach that his son loved football and had worked hard to reach his current level of play. While the kid didn't expect any special treatment, he just wanted a fair opportunity to compete for *his* position. The coach replied, "I won't give him that opportunity." That answer was so ridiculous; you might want to reread it to make sure you fully understand how far off the rails this coach went. That statement was so wrong for so many reasons. I hope you can see that there is absolutely no place in high school sports for that mindset. (I know one high school principal who would have fired that coach on the spot for taking that approach to the players on his team. – See the Preface.)

For the next three years, this coach worked with this one class and his young quarterback (not his son this time) in anticipation of this class's senior season. This man was coaching for his resume and his shot at a state championship several years away. The players who were not going to be around for that season were shuffled aside, regardless of who the best players were.

Along the way, many quality players were benched in favor of younger ones. One displaced player, with limited experience and exposure, went on to play Division III college football, started three years, and was academic All-America for three years.

Possibly the greatest injustice was done to a quiet, unassuming defensive back. In looking at the roster before the weaker class's senior season, I saw a name I didn't recognize so I asked one of the players who this other player was. His answer broke my heart. He said, "He could be pretty good, but he'll never get a chance." This kid had the misfortune of being in the wrong class when the wrong coach came to town. By not giving this *quality* player a chance, do you really think this coach was interested in developing his players and putting his best team on the field each season? Nope. That next season was the only one that mattered to this coach and his resume. You got it: another example of *what to avoid!*

More on this same coach…(yes, there's even more) During this build-up for the magical senior season, the coach chose as quarterback a 5' 11", 170 pound 40% passer ahead of a 6' 3", 225 pound 60% passer who was one year older. The little guy was the fastest player on the team; the other kid was the third fastest so there wasn't a big speed difference there. Remember, they run a triple option offense so speed is important.

The smaller player could not read a field, could not execute the option, and could not hit a wide-open receiver, but he did have a strong arm. The problem was that his accuracy was so bad; he couldn't throw the football in the ocean from standing on the shore so his arm strength was irrelevant. Also, he was not big enough to succeed with the tough,

25

inside running plays, which is a necessity in this offense. But he was fast! His speedy, swivel hipped style of running was perfect for the outside runs that a triple option offense provides for a running back.

The other player ran a very well timed option, read the field extremely well, had pinpoint accuracy with his passes, and was able to run the tough, inside yards on quarterback keepers in addition to having breakaway speed for the outside opportunities. The only thing he couldn't do that the little guy could do, was play one more season. That was the key for this coach. The only year that mattered was that next season when the bulk of his players would be seniors and it didn't matter who the better players were between now and then.

I understand that some of the best teams at any level get that way in part by utilizing the same players year after year. A team can become quite unified as it gains more experience playing the same players as one unit. I have seen my own teams gain huge advantages over their opponents because the players played together long enough to know what each other would do in certain situations. It goes without saying that the longer you can have the same players work together, the more in sync they will be. Still, the best players have earned the right to play. A good coach will find other techniques to get his team to reach its potential without benching better players in favor of keeping that one age group together. When a coach shows favoritism, he erodes his credibility and that has a negative impact on the pipeline of players wanting to play in his program.

At this school, typically the varsity team, with the JV team included, consisted of roughly 25 seniors, 25 juniors, and 25 sophomores. This very talented class followed a very lean class so one year; the makeup of the team was 13 seniors, 50 juniors, and 25 sophomores. The football program was building to a crescendo for that championship season. That's great. After all, winning championships is why we compete and keep score. Still, players compete for playing time and you should never take away their opportunity to compete.

You have just read a couple of, "How Not To…," descriptions of coaching and developing a program. In your coaching endeavors, do not let yourself be that kind of coach. You owe it to the kids and the quality of your program to look past your resume. It is not about you: it is about your players. You are influencing young lives. The effect you have on them will not be apparent for a number of years, but that impact will be longer lasting and far more important than the sport itself.

Please don't misunderstand. I am as competitive as anyone you'll meet but I still believe that the best you can do is to coach each player to the best of his ability – without regard for your resume. By doing that, you will better serve your players; you will win more games year in and year out; players will *want to play for you* thereby keeping the pipeline of talent full; and the integrity of your program will remain strong. In a nutshell, your resume will be better for having taken the "kids first" approach rather than the "me first" approach. Anyone see any irony here?

I am very dogmatic about why coaches should or should not coach. As you can tell, I believe the players' wellbeing comes first. As a coach, you are not there to show favoritism to your child, your buddies' children, or the sons of the good-looking moms. Your responsibility is not to your resume either. Your responsibility is to your players. If you do things right by your players, your resume will reflect that.

You need a very wide altruistic streak in your makeup if you are going to be the best coach possible. Remember, if you are not genuine in your devotion to your players and their wellbeing, they will know. If you bring the right attitude, you will give yourself the best opportunity to have a successful program and ultimately the best resume.

Footnote: For that senior football season, of the 50 juniors returning to play for a championship caliber team, only 28 came back to the team for their senior season. Think about that. How many high school seniors do you know that would walk away from a possible state championship in any sport? That sort of effect can be felt throughout your pipeline if you mishandle your players - and the success of your program will reflect that. That statistic speaks volumes about that coach. You guessed it: another example of *what to avoid!*

Be The
Ultimate
Sports Coach

II. Now that I've Gotten Myself into this Mess, Where do I Start?

This one's easy; start at the beginning. No, seriously; start out as if the kids, parents, etc. never have been involved in any sort of organized sport at all. Chances are, they have been, but maybe they've been at the mercy of one of the types of coaches we met in chapter one…and we don't want to repeat any of those errors, right?

Also, you need to start at the beginning with yourself. What the heck do I mean by that? Get involved. (Duh, right?) If you are coaching in youth leagues, consider coaching more than one sport. If this is not a good option for you, but your child might play more than one sport, by all means go to as many practices and games as possible. There are many reasons why this seems obvious but I am not here to preach to you about how to raise your own child. As far as coaching goes, the more you see other coaches work, the more you will learn – good and bad – and all of this new knowledge will help you to be the best coach you can be.

We are looking at this strictly from the perspective of you becoming a good coach. Watch the kids. Learn their skills. Learn their temperaments. The more you know about all the kids, the better able you will be to select a cohesive team in your sport and to help each player reach the best of his potential. More on this later.

Now, back to the other people. First of all, you want to educate everyone about the way you will be doing things. This may be a far cry from what they're used to in this topsy-turvy world of youth league sports. Secondly, there are so many boneheads out there coaching youth-league sports that you want to begin to eliminate any preconceived notions these people may have that you too are, in fact, a bonehead. (Hopefully, you don't inadvertently reinforce that notion.) You can also begin to give your league a positive image within your community with a well thought out approach to the monumental task before you.

Whenever I called my players' parents to inform them of the first practice, I always made a point of requiring an adult to accompany the player. If a parent, grandparent, aunt, or uncle was not available, an older sibling could do in a pinch. Yes, this sounds like a major pain in the pitooty (another euphemism), but if you do this, you will avoid many sources of trouble as the novelty of the season wears off and your honeymoon period with the parents ends. You *do* want the parents on your side.

If any parents ever questioned the importance of their attendance at this practice/meeting, I simply pointed out that it was integral to the overall success of what we would try to accomplish that season for their precious Little Johnny. That usually was enough to bring them into the fold. If they still were not convinced, I would gently point out that with all of the time the other coaches and I would be investing in the team, it was not unreasonable to ask them to attend just one measly practice. (Yes, I could be a real so-and-so at times.)

Write out your team rules but do not give them to parents until after you have read them and discussed them with the group. Make your rules simple, something like: 'This is what I expect from you and your kid(s); this is what you can expect from me.' You will quickly learn, much to your surprise that these captains of industry, these highly respected doctors, lawyers, and even teachers won't knock you over with their innate intelligence. When it comes to their own children, somehow common sense gets left by the wayside.

Again: **DO NOT PASS OUT ANY INFORMATION UNTIL YOU HAVE READ AND EXPLAINED IT TO THE PARENTS FIRST!** It is important that the parents actually hear what you have to say and ask any questions on the spot. This will give everyone the opportunity to hear the concerns of others and it could possibly spark additional questions. If they have their collective noses buried in the papers you have given them, they won't hear a word you're saying and you'll waste a lot of time repeating yourself. And since you've only written a basic outline, what you say is more important than what is written on the paper.

Also, be prepared for that one parent who is so special that no matter how all-inclusive a specific line item is on your list, their personal situation will be the exception to the rule. Never mind that in the history of all sports played everywhere, their exception has never occurred – and won't occur this season either. The important point here is for this person to hear himself or herself talk and thereby demonstrate how important he or she is. Let 'em talk and go on. (It will be difficult to keep from rolling your eyes during this self-aggrandizing speech, but please try.)

Cover your rain and snow rules if applicable. Obviously, some common sense comes into play here, but there will be many borderline cases so you will need to cover them as best as you can. With snow, it's fairly easy because if we are concerned with a school-sponsored league and school is cancelled, the buildings won't be open. If the snow is that bad, you don't want people diving in it anyway.

What do you do in case of rain? Whatever your policies are, define them. In basketball, it's a nonfactor. In baseball, it was tough to do anything unless it was a very light drizzle. In football, the limiting factor was lightning. For my teams, if there was no lightning, there was practice. Many times, my team was the only one practicing on a rainy afternoon.

Put in writing your practice and game schedules. Sometimes you won't have all of this information, but give them all you have as soon as possible with a promise to provide them with additional information as soon as it becomes available. When you give them this season's, "bible," promise them that what you have just given them, written in ink, etched in stone, and signed in blood *will change*. Everyone involved will be trying to juggle their jobs, other children and their schedules, and myriad other distractions to your all-important season's schedule so you have to let them know that you will do your best to keep them informed of any changes at the earliest possible opportunity.

After this initial meeting has come and gone, and you are trying to move forward with the season, always make sure you have extra copies of these most important, all-inclusive information sheets and schedules with you at all times. You will be amazed that the parents aren't any more organized than the players and therefore will frequently come to you with the old, "…my dog ate my homework; can I have another copy…?" story.

Communication is one of the biggest keys to a successful completion of the season. You will expect the same communication from your players and their parents so you must set the tone from the beginning. Remember that part about leading by example? …And that other part about teaching the parents about responsibility? We've done all of this hard work and we haven't even swung the first bat, bounced the first ball, or made the first tackle!

Again, communication is so important to having a cooperative, working relationship. You want these parents and families on your side so that when you have to chew on little Johnny's tail because, after thirty-umpteen explanations, he still hasn't gotten it right, they at least give you the benefit of the doubt. Establish the procedures you will follow regarding any issues that will affect the families and let them know the procedures they will need to follow as well.

When doing this, be sure you have itemized any necessary penalties the players may suffer for missing practices, games, etc. Obviously, there will be certain family situations that come up unexpectedly and you can't be so rigid that you expect the entire world to stop and revolve around your schedule. But you also need to have guidelines in place. Doing this will eliminate a lot of confused players and upset parents. (You'll never eliminate all of the angry parents, but this is a good start.)

******

I had a situation arise one year involving some players who apparently got confused about what was expected. I was involved in a football youth league for seven years. I held various offices in the league and positions on the board as we changed the league from a glorified

35

neighborhood get together to a well-run league with honest-to-goodness by-laws and stuff.

We had a lower league for kids aged 6-9 and an upper league for kids aged 10-12. There was a specific minimum number of plays we were required to play each child during each half. Coaches could schedule a maximum of three practices per week. In general, the kids were expected to be at each practice or the coach was not obligated to play them in the game. If players missed practices, coaches then had the latitude to administer that rule based on their specific team rules. Excused absences did not affect a player's eligibility.

I covered this rule and my interpretation of it during our first practice/meeting. Because of this and other rules that would affect players during the season, I was very adamant about the adults' attendance to this first practice. Keep in mind that you are setting a good example for these kids and you have to be flexible when you prioritize…i. e., football doesn't always come first. I know that may sound like heresy to a dedicated football coach, but let's take a moment to dry those tears and get back on message here.

We're talking youth league football (or even high school in some instances) here – basically anything lower than college sports when they really become a business and the rules change. For our purposes, there are more important things for these kids and their families such as school, church, Aunt Edna's 100th birthday, and well, you get the idea. I know that sounds blasphemous to many a sports fanatic, but you've got to be realistic.

My players were required to be at all scheduled practices during the week, usually three, unless they called before the practice to let me know of their upcoming absence. This is as much about teaching the kids (and their parents) responsibility as allowing you to plan your practices.

Example: I once coached a pair of brothers whose dad usually stayed to watch football practices. As usual, they got there in good time to start practice but only one brother came to begin stretching and warming up. I went to the father and asked about the other brother. Dad told me he was in the truck finishing his homework. FANTASTIC! This was a great teaching moment. I applauded the dad and, of course, the child was not punished for missing part of the practice.

Since the dad told me the boy had plenty of time to complete the work at home, but was horsing around and just didn't do it, we took this teaching opportunity one step further. When I commended the boy for doing his homework before practice, I made it clear to him that it is a rare occasion that a kid would have so much homework that he couldn't finish it after school and before practice time at 5:30. (I was fully aware that he didn't have very much homework, but I didn't want to bust his chops; just get my message across. I told him that if this became a habit, he would begin missing some playing time. He got the message and did well in school and for the team and we never had that problem again. I also had one set of parents firmly on my side because of my support of education and their decision to hold the player out of practice until the homework was finished.

Sometimes I got home from practice to find a message on my answering machine. That was perfectly acceptable, as we don't always answer every phone call and this was before cell phones. It isn't perfect because, as a coach, you do plan on working on certain things with certain players and it helps to know in advance which players will be at practice. As long as the child and/or parent made the effort to show some responsibility to the team, I figured that was fair enough.

What are acceptable excuses? Among them would be illness, confirmation class, too much homework, and no transportation. You will also have many school functions that you must respect. You may have your best pitcher miss a game because of Music Night or another key player missing because of an Open House. You just have to swallow your ego and realize that your sports team takes a back seat to these things.

I once had a player who couldn't reach me by phone, so he rode his bicycle to practice to tell me that his grandmother (his caregiver at the time), was sick and he wouldn't be able to stay for practice. He had to take care of her. When he left, I was speechless. This young man didn't have the picture perfect home structure, but he had enough self-discipline to do this. That was one of those wonderful moments that you get to experience when you get involved with youth sports. By the way, he did not get punished for missing a practice.

* * * * * *

My last year in youth football, we had ***the team to beat.*** I spent the entire season biting my lip to keep from letting it slip how good my team was. I used positive reinforcement to build their skill levels, but I didn't dare tell them how much better they were than the other teams in the league. I could write pages and pages waxing eloquence about how good that team was and just how fantastic that group of kids was, but that isn't the point here. (Disappointed, huh?) Don't worry though; I *will* go into the minutiae of the makings of this team.

We were in the playoffs and scheduled to face the only team in the league to have beaten us. It rained and rained and rained all week. We were as happy as could be because the other team had the fastest player on the field and in a close game in youth football – any level of football really, as long as there is another snap of the ball to be had, the fastest player on the field could find his way to the end zone. That muddy slop could be our friend come Saturday.

The weather that week was dreadful for everything except football teams and ducks. The temperature throughout the week was in the 70s with a solid rain each day. There was never a real storm and therefore we never saw any lightning. In other words, practice went as scheduled...*for my team anyway*.

We were the only team in the entire league to practice. O. k., our team was the only one with a coach who was a couple of sandwiches shy of a full picnic basket, but our kids had a ball. Sixteen of them did anyway. Four did not show up all week, probably due to a massive outbreak of broken fingers I guess, because none of them could dial a phone. All week. No phone calls. Not one of them. (Remember my team rules.)

Any parent who has ever had to scream and *scream* and **scream** at their kids to come into the house to get out of the rain could imagine the fun these boys had. They sloshed through drills and plays all week and took much of our practice field home with them in the form of mud on their uniforms. I have never seen happier faces at practices - among the players. Their parents were not exactly overjoyed at the idea of sitting through a rainy practice and then having their kids get in their cars for the rides home. But we were ready for game day and that's the important thing, right?

Footnote: One father worked for a heating and air company. He had in his company van, a huge roll of plastic. Each day, at the end of practice, the players lined up at the back of his van and he cut large pieces of plastic for the players to sit on and thereby protect their parents' cars. He got the MVP award for that week. It's great when parents become this involved.

The weather on game day was more of the same. My players were well prepared for this sloppy mess because they had three days of playing in it. In any athletic endeavor, proper footwork is extremely important. There are specific rules to follow if you are a lineman, a quarterback, a soccer player, tennis player, etc. My kids learned these things.

Some of these rules change when playing in the mud. One of the most important things is to keep your feet closer together. Don't get me wrong; you don't want your linemen getting their feet so close together that they tip over sideways, but they need to keep their feet under the weight of their bodies. Otherwise, they might do the splits, and not the graceful, coordinated kind: the kind that look like a newborn deer that can't quite stand.

Runners need to take shorter strides, again keeping their weight over the feet. Players can cut much quicker with shorter strides. They are harder to knock off of their feet by would-be tacklers who are also slipping and sliding in a delightfully muddy field. (Are you questioning

41

my use of the descriptive term, "...delightfully muddy?") Have you ever known a football player who wasn't absolutely ecstatic at the prospect of playing on a warm, wet, muddy, sloppy field?

Our quarterback was a tall kid but not skinny. He had good weight to him to go with his very quick feet. He learned the "short step" lesson very well. I'd like to take credit, but it was his older brother, also a football player, who taught him that technique. It served him very well throughout his playing career.

Fast forward: This kid went on to score three touchdowns in one quarter and four in one half of a mud game while he was in high school. It was comical watching him run like a sped up Charlie Chaplin with his big body and his little bitty steps. That is, until you watched him cut as the other players slid by face down in the muck. That's when you could really see how effective that technique can be.

And now, back to our playoff game. As the game wore on, we established a 6-0 halftime lead. I used the sixteen players who practiced all week. I did include the other four on special teams: kickoffs, kick returns, punts, and punt returns, which, by rule, I did not have to do. In the first half, that only involved two plays: the opening kickoff and the kickoff following our touchdown. (There were no punts.) Please understand that the magnitude of the game had nothing to do with these players not playing; it was simply a rules violation.

In the second half, both teams continued to play in the slop. It was difficult to tell which players were on which teams with all of the brown uniforms. As I prowled the sidelines intently watching the action, I got the sense that I was being stared at and followed. Don't you just hate that feeling?

Our league sideline rules provided a buffer zone that helped in just such occasions. The players had to stay between the thirty yard lines; coaches could go as far as the twenty-five, leaving a five yard 'coaches only' zone. (This was my little safety zone that I could use to get at least five yards worth of fresh, "unchildcluttered" air. As much as I loved the little knuckleheads, sometimes you've just gotta get away from them and clear your head. (Just ask any teacher.))

Anyway, I'm standing in my little safety zone and I can feel some eyes just boring into the back of my head. I turned around to see what looked like my own private little bird nest with four little ones all looking at me as if waiting for me to present them with a worm. One of them, the designated spokesman of the group spoke up. He asked, "When do we get to play?"

I sort of thought that might be their approach but still; the directness of it caught me off guard. I can never remember being as angry at any of my players as I was at that moment. Oh, sure, it was great that they wanted to play. Every kid who ever plays a sport should want to be

43

in the game every single play, but sometimes in any sport, for a whole variety of reasons that is not the case.

This was in the fourth quarter of the semifinal game and we were clinging to a 6-0 lead. Not much that we are trying to do is working in this slop, but fortunately our opponents were playing on the same field. What upset me about these boys was that their collective attitude showed that I had failed.

I had failed in all that I had taught them about attitude toward the team. That they were so involved in their own little world of how much playing time they would get as individuals instead of looking at how they could best help their team was what first got to me. The second was the fact that they had the audacity, (even before they could spell audacity), to ask about playing time when none of them had been to practice all week, nor had they followed one of the basic team rules that we had covered on many occasions. That dreaded and cumbersome phone call rule.

As soon as the question was out of the boy's mouth, I looked very sternly (euphemism here: I was flat out mad!) at each of them as I asked, in a very terse manner, "How many practices did any of you attend this week and how many phone calls did I get?" Unbelievably, no; I guess I should say – predictably - they all had shocked looks on their faces. Phone call? Huh? Gee, Mr. Obvious, I never made the connection. I don't know if that was because they could tell that I really was rather perturbed with them or that they were somehow unaware that the rules applied to them.

That was the lesson that I wanted taught and I think it got through to them that time. Rules are rules – for everybody. I was never confronted or even questioned by any of those kids' parents. That's how I know I got through to the kids. You see, a child will usually slant things in his favor when a parent asks him things such as, "Why didn't you play?" When Little Johnny tells Big Daddy he doesn't know why he didn't play, Big Daddy wants to find out for himself. Depending on Big Daddy's temperament and I. Q. points, the coach could find himself in hot water. In this case, the rules were spelled out quite clearly in the beginning and our team had already seen how they worked.

******

We had one previous instance during the season when a player skipped a couple of practices. His absences were unexcused so he did not play in the next game. He was one of our biggest starting linemen, and a very good one at that. Let me tell you, every mobile 176 lb. lineman you can get in a 10 – 12 year old youth football league is very valuable.

I wanted him on the field, but rules are rules. The players saw that he was valuable to the team, but he still had to follow the rules or suffer the consequences. On one hand, it hurt the team that he was not on the field. On the other hand, it did the team a lot of good because the players (most of them anyway) understood that the rules were to be followed even if you were a starter. It was a great lesson for the players to learn at this early age. It also helped our team come together because we had to play a non-starter on offense and another one on defense to replace the benched behemoth. They got valuable experience that came back to help us during the playoff run that year.

I didn't know it then, but benching that player probably kept me out of trouble with the other parents during the mud game. You never try to use one situation to set up another situation, but it happens and in this case, it was a blessing. Rules are rules and they have to be enforced equivalently. I say equivalently instead of equally because there will always be differences in some situations, but as long as things are equivalent, you won't have too many complaints.

* * * * * *

Now that you've covered all of the season's procedures and expectations with the parents, you can get started with the players.

Sometimes I include an abbreviated version of what I tell the players when I address the parents.

What I tell the players is this. I am the easiest coach to play for, that they will ever experience. Why? Because I have only two rules. The first rule is; when coaches talk, players' ears are open and their mouths are shut. It doesn't matter which coach it is, or even a team manager; players' ears are open and their mouths are shut. The second rule is that players must try as hard as they can, within the bounds of the rules, to do everything that is asked of them.

Basically, everything that comes up will fall under one of these two rules. We try to cover everything they need to know so when they have a question, it is probably because they weren't paying attention when it was discussed. Reinforce the importance of rule number one.

The second rule is really all encompassing. If they give the effort, that's all you can ask. You can't expect players to be perfect but if they listen to what they're told and try as hard as they can, that's really about all you can ask from them, no matter what the age. Remember, getting your players to reach their potential is your goal and it is the best you can possibly do. You can't ask for miracles and supermen. You are trying to drive each player to reach his potential and then get the team to the best of its potential. That's the best you can do.

I adapted my approach to the beginning of any season to a communication technique my high school speech teacher espoused. He taught his classes that when giving a speech, tell your audience what you're going to tell them; tell them; and then tell them what you told them. Don't worry, it sounded stupid to me too, until I realized that he was right.

I have followed that philosophy my entire adult life in many situations. When writing a letter of application for a job, you tell the reader you are writing because you want to ask for the job; tell him or her why you deserve it and ask for the job; then summarize by thanking him or her for giving you the opportunity to prove yourself by giving you the job for which you've just asked. (See how difficult it is to deal with, "him or her," instead of sticking with just the one pronoun?)

If you use that approach with the parents at the beginning, you will smooth out a lot of potential wrinkles before they even occur. Please understand that parents can make or break your pleasant coaching experience as well as the success of the entire season. Spend the extra time up front and the parents will be on your side. You'll look forward to many more fun and fruitful seasons.

Be The
Ultimate
Sports Coach

III. I Know More Than They Do; This'll Be Easy

Now let's figure out how to teach these kids something. Actually, the longer I watched during that first season before I got involved, the more I realized that those coaches I was watching knew very little about baseball…and this opinion coming from someone whose weakest sport is baseball. I also figured that since I was a salesman and actually got paid to communicate with people, I might be able to explain the fundamentals of the sport in a way that they could understand.

The ability to communicate is a huge asset at all levels of coaching, maybe even more important at the high school level when the teenage mind is hard at work thinking about anything except what you are trying to explain; and more often than not, those thoughts are centered around members of the opposite sex. Surprise! *Surprise!* *Surprise!*

It took a few seasons to fine tune some of my teaching techniques and some of the phrases that would cause the light bulb of understanding to pop on in the minds of these eager little ballplayers. One of the driving thoughts in the back of my mind as I mustered the courage to undertake the arduous task of coaching young players was, "I know more that they do; this'll be easy." How naïve I was in my relative coaching youth.

As I came to realize, if you can paint a word picture about a concept that is so foreign to a child as tagging up on a fly ball, - or in basketball; opening to the ball to prevent a back door pass, or in football; containing the outside sweep, - in such a way that the child actually understands it, you can certainly describe the merits of your company's latest innovative product to some unsuspecting purchasing agent who presumably has at least a fourth grade education. Coaching kids actually helped me become a much better salesman. But I digress.

In all of my coaching, I incorporate that old speech writing formula. Tell them what you're going to tell them; tell them; then tell them what you told them. Let's use football as an example. If I am teaching them a play, I will tell them about the play we are going to learn. Next, I go through each player's responsibility and tasks. Lastly, we put it all together so they can see how integral each player's job is to the play. *Tell them what you're going to tell them; tell them; then tell them what you told them.* Works every time. (O. k., usually.)

* * * * * *

Here are some specific things to remember about addressing the kids. First, you may absolutely, positively never ever use any profanity. Regardless of the age of the children or the language their parents use to get them to clean their rooms, you will be held to a higher standard and will find yourself incurring the wrath of some hostile soccer mom if you curse at her poor little child….no matter how badly the #$@&%*! child deserves it.

Depending on your personal habits, training yourself to avoid saying the no-nos will have varying degrees of difficulty. When you first start being around the kids, choose a couple of expressions you want to use for emphasis. You will use euphemisms a lot in coaching youth sports. Gosh darn it, dadgummit, fudge cookies, or whatever you feel comfortable with is fine. (I once drew a fifteen yard penalty for saying, "Dagnab it!" as I walked away from an official to drown my frustrations in my Mountain Dew. I guess euphemisms don't always produce the desired results. Go figure.) Regardless, you will be surprised at how quickly you can discipline yourself to speak as you would in church, as it were.

Often, I will tell the parents in the first practice meeting that I have a no profanity policy. That always scores points with them, plus it implies that they need to behave accordingly. I then go on to tell them the one exception to that rule. In the unlikely event that I would ever need to provide transportation home for a player, that policy is suspended. After all, with all of the idiots driving on the roads these days, it is practically a necessity to curse while driving. That usually gets a chuckle and relaxes people while I am broaching a potentially touchy subject.

The second thing to remember is to consider the age of the kids and use words they know. In basketball, don't tell a six-year-old kid to maintain his position on the block and deny the entry pass. He doesn't know 'maintain,' where the 'block' is, or what it means to deny an entry pass. This goes back to the concept that you can't yell at a player for not knowing something unless you have taught that concept. Remember, do not assume that since a player has had a specific number of birthdays, that he knows certain things. You don't know what his previous coaches have taught him.

Vocabulary is one of those things that you can teach very quickly as you go along. Do *not* just ask who does not know what xyz means. Your players, especially boys, will be too embarrassed to admit that they do not know something so they won't fess up. Try this: "O. k., when you set up on the block…," (as you are going to the block), point to the square on the floor and define it as, "The Block." It takes all of five seconds and you'll be surprised how much time and effort little things like this will save you down the road.

Continuing on this same train of thought, as a part of your teaching, as you introduce new concepts to your eager young players, define the new term for the new technique you are teaching. Do this regardless of the age of the players. I know that sounds ridiculously simple, but trust me; your players' previous coaches probably have not done this.

So many coaches assume that, because the players are a certain age, they know certain things. That is not necessarily the case. I've seen many high school coaches start in the middle of the book when the players haven't learned the first chapter yet. Remember, you have no idea what your players' previous coaches were like.

Defining terms. What an odd place to start. It sounds simple, but to draw a contrast, try asking a high school senior to explain the defensive alignments his football team uses. You will hear terms such as Monster, Bear, Red Dog, Panther, or whatever other specially defined terms his team uses. Some of these terms may be universal in the world of football, but if you are not in that arena so to speak, (Notice the nifty play on words?), you won't know the lingo and you can get lost rather easily. Why? *Because nobody has defined the terms for you.* Do your players and yourself a favor; define even the simplest terms.

For example, I once was coaching an 8th grade middle school basketball team. After a couple of weeks of practice, I noticed some of the kids seemed lost. As it turned out; they didn't know the basic spots on the floor. Nobody had ever specifically defined terms like the block, the elbow, etc. For a while, players can fake their way through not knowing exactly what the terms mean but sooner or later it catches up to them. Plus, think how much easier it will be for you to teach more complex concepts if you all understand the same basic language.

Remember, the children you are coaching have knowledge bases ranging from nothing (T-ballers) up to not nearly as much as they think they know (Teenagers). You do know more about the sport than they do; now you have to communicate it to them and bring them up to your level of understanding. Plus, you can't yell at them for not knowing something unless you have taught it to them and they still don't remember. (Let's be honest; yelling at kids is one of the perks of the job, right?)

For example, do not assume a high school sophomore knows how to tackle just because he's been playing football for four years. Show him just as you would a six year old, and when you've seen him perform it perfectly and he looks at you like you're an idiot for being so simplistic, you can assume he knows how to tackle and you can move on. I used tackling as an example because of the seriousness of injuries that can occur if proper techniques are not used. Specifically with tackling, never assume kids know anything until you've explained in very precise terms how to do it and worked with them to perfect their technique.

Remember too, that a kid never wants to speak up and admit to a coach – especially not in front of his teammates – that he doesn't understand. This is true no matter what age your players are. Maybe it's the male ego rearing its ugly head. Whatever the reason, it is a simple fact that the vast majority of your players will be embarrassed to speak up about not knowing something, especially in front of the whole team.

When teaching anything, you have to make sure you explain your point in easily understood language. Since you have probably had children of the age you'll be coaching, you can use your own children's vocabulary level at that age as a reference point when selecting appropriately small words.

******

My first season coaching youth league football was spent with 6, 7, 8, and 9 year olds. I assisted a young gentleman who played college and semi-pro football but, was 24 years old and single with no kids. I knew nothing about teaching football and he knew nothing about talking to small children. We were a match made in heaven.

I spent the first half of the season learning from him the principles and techniques he wanted to teach the players. Many times, I looked into these empty little helmets and saw that the lights were most definitely not on. I then translated what he said into little bitty six-year-old words so that the youngest and least experienced player would know exactly what we were teaching. At first, the coach gave me these odd looks that said, "What are you doing? I just told them that."

It didn't take him long to catch on to what I was doing. Eventually he would ask me, before addressing the team, how to explain a new concept. (i. e., How do you explain the concept that to contain an area in an open field, you need to break down prior to attempting the tackle?) Notice the foreign words to young players, "*contain* and *break down.*"

A few extra minutes to explain those terms in detail paid dividends for us down the road. It also gave these boys some pride in having learned some big bad football terms. (Have you ever seen the pride *and* simultaneous frustration a seven-year-old displays when explaining to his mother what he learned at football practice? You'll see him roll his eyes when his mother – who, in his mind, is now on her way to becoming one of the stupidest people on the face of the earth – doesn't understand.) This peewee leaguer is well on his way to becoming a teenager.

******

Another thing you will learn very quickly is that practices need to be fast paced. By that I mean that you have to keep the players' minds occupied. They have to be doing something or thinking about doing something. If not, depending on the age of the players, they will be kicking dirt in the shoes of the next player, flicking another player's ear, or thinking about Susie from chemistry class.

Do not try to shoot from the hip with your practices. Make a practice plan. Plan your drills complete with the amount of time spent on each drill and water breaks. Print a copy for each coach. Be sure all coaches understand that the practice plan is subject to change at a moment's notice. If you're a little (or a lot) high strung, you might get upset after spending all of your time preparing that practice plan and then nobody follows it. You can't show that. It'll affect your team's perception of you. In logical sequence, it follows that this will affect your ability to lead the team when it really counts.

When you're forced to spend extra time on one drill, do not try to rush, rush, rush to get back on schedule. This creates a frenetic, panicked pace and it is very unsettling to the players. This is not helpful when trying to get your message to sink in to these empty brains.

Also, you want your players to know that you are always in control. You are running the practice; the practice is not running you. One of the things you will be teaching is that your players need to remain calm during games so they can function at a high level. By conducting yourself properly during a chaotic practice, you are teaching by example. This will pay you dividends many times over throughout the season and it will benefit the kids on future teams and in later life.

After you've blown your time schedule, which will probably happen every practice, look at exactly how much time you've lost. Look at the remaining drills on the schedule and find one or more that you can skip that will balance the time constraint and may not be super critical to that day's practice. Be sure that the omitted drill is included in the next practice. In football and basketball it is somewhat easier to maintain a schedule than in baseball.

No matter how much planning you put into it, baseball practice drills always take longer. You always have to chase balls and usually it takes a while to get enough decent pitches for each batter to hit (or miss), etc. On paper, it doesn't look so tough, but go through a few practices and you'll see what I mean. You won't even know the time has disappeared until it's too late to recover. Keep an extra close watch on the time in baseball so you can make your changes as soon as they are needed.

******

I remember one football practice with a very strong team full of veterans. It seems that on this day, every one of them drank goofy juice at lunch. I don't know what the problem was, but none of them could focus. (Hey, look! A squirrel.)

The first thing on my practice schedule was teaching three new plays. It was all I could do to get them to focus long enough to get into the proper formation, walk through a play, then run it at full speed one time. You'll never guess their reaction when they ran the first play correctly. That's right, they asked almost in unison; "What do we do now?" Being the jerk that I am, I told them to run it again. How cruel could I be? Fortunately, it comes naturally.

We managed to get through those three plays without too much trouble, but only because I knew more than they did. (Notice how I keep coming back to the title of the chapter? I'm clever that way.) The method I used to keep their squirrely little minds harnessed was to tell them I had other things planned that I knew they would really enjoy, but first; they had to learn those plays and run them right three times apiece. A little bribery never hurts when your intentions are pure.

The promise of the reward kept them focused just long enough to perfect the new plays. (Barely!) I did not want to let this practice deteriorate into me yelling at them for not being serious because, after all, we all have days like that. Surprisingly, I kept my cool and as soon as we got through the plays, I set up some one-on-one tackling drills. My practice plan was down the drain that day, but I knew one way for us to have a productive and enjoyable practice.

These kids absolutely loved tackling. That was my ace in the hole. I started with a basic one-on-one tackling drill. Then I changed the angles of approach, added a blocker and an extra defender, and anything else I could think of to change things slightly without involving too much concentration on the part of the players because, quite frankly, on this day they didn't have it. I had to make my alterations to the basic drill very minor so I could get it done quickly, and thereby maintain some semblance of an attention span. (There's that squirrel again.)

We tackled for an hour that day. Those kids had a blast and went home exhausted. (Parents always like that because a tired – but happy – kid is always cooperative.) I was able to turn a potential disaster of a practice into one of the most fun – and productive - ones they had all season.

I was able to do this without them knowing that I threw out almost the entire practice plan because they were just too goofy to work with that day. They got better at something they loved and we had a very valuable practice. We were far and away the best tackling team in the league because we spent more time on it than any other team. I can promise you that no team ever approached a solid hour of tackling during a single practice – maybe not in an entire week!

By midway through the season, of the 22 players on the team, 16 were strong tacklers. The players also had varying degrees of other skills, but I had 16 that I could play on defense without hesitation. In youth football, 16 out of 22 is an incredible percentage of capable tacklers. (One player was injured so I really had only five players to "hide" somewhere.) Most teams were lucky to have six or eight solid football players. We were clearly the superior tackling team in the league. It was so evident that the other coaches frequently told me that throughout the season. Oh yeah, we won the championship that year. Let's see. Superior tackling leads to the Championship. Coincidence or correlation? Gee, Mr. Obvious, did you make the connection?

* * * * * *

Please understand that not every clever little tactic that I used worked quite as successfully as this one. I'm not too vain to admit when something doesn't work. You keep a mental file cabinet of analogies, illustrative examples, and tales of teams past that you can draw upon when the right situation arises. Not all of them work as planned so sometimes one goes in the, "Do Not Use," file.

******

One such illustration involved jai alai. I had a basketball team that was just not getting the message. Half of them were glued to my every word and tried really hard to do what I asked. The other half of the team ran around like their pants were on fire and they couldn't find the lake.

I tried to hold the line and run through my practice plans just as I had done with many teams before and would do with many more teams. These goofballs just – squirrel – wouldn't stay focused. Finally, one day, I had had enough.

I could either go rudikazooty on them or I could maintain my composure and tell them an illustrative story. (Ru' dee ka zoo' tee. It's a highly technical coaching term.) I chose the latter.

I stopped practice and said very enthusiastically, "Hey guys, I've got a great idea. I have some equipment out in my car. I'm going to go bring it in and we're going to play a different game. It's called jai alai."

The boys all looked at me rather confused - as if half of them didn't live in a perpetual state of confusion anyway. Just like with a great comedy team, one of the players took my slow pitch, spoke up and said, "Jai alai? What's that? How do you play?"

My reply, "Exactly. You have no idea how to play jai alai so you asked me how to play. You also have no idea how to play basketball, but you will not listen to what I am trying to teach you."

The half of the team that had triple digit IQs and didn't really need to hear this message understood it; the goofballs on the team had no clue that this message was directed at them. O. k., so I filed the "Jai Alai" story in the, "Do Not Use," file, never to be trotted out again except in instances like this when I am illustrating the, "How Not To…," chapter.

* * * * * *

Another area that needs a lot of emphasis in the world of athletics is the subject of competition. Whether you are coaching young players who may be getting their first exposure to competitive sports or older players who should already know how to compete, you still need to spend ample time on this subject. For the younger players, the reasons are obvious. For the older players, remember I've already pointed out that there are a lot of subpar coaches out there. You may need to correct some damage done by a previous coach.

This is a very serious part of the whole sports world so do not gloss over this. Do not assume, because of the age or experience of the players, that they understand that there is a right way to compete and there is a wrong way to compete. The phrase I always use is, "Clean, fair, and legal." (With apologies to my elementary English teachers. I realize those should be adverbs not adjectives, but you just can't get the same emphasis by saying, "Cleanly, fairly, and legally.")

******

When my son was in high school, the middle linebacker on his team was a fantastic athlete who had accepted a major college football scholarship. This kid was clearly head and shoulders better than any other player on the field – in every game they played. In one particular game, on nearly every play, the opposing team's center went head hunting and tried to take out the linebacker's knees.

Going down field to block a player at the knees is illegal and extremely dirty. He was called for a penalty only twice, but he should have been called every play until disqualification was in order. This is not a case of, "Did he or didn't he do it on purpose?" This was clearly an orchestrated move and I would bet the ranch that the player did not come up with the idea on his own.

I can't say for sure if his coach taught the player to do it or if his father did, but I can promise you; the player was not the brains behind this tactic. The linebacker was a man among boys and taking him out of the game would have given a huge advantage to the other team. Still, you just don't resort to these (or any other) dirty tactics.

Fortunately, they were unsuccessful in injuring our player and the stud went on to enjoy his college career and utilize his $120,000+ scholarship. Regardless of the stakes of the specific game; why would you ever want to deliberately try to injure another player; take away his scholarship; ruin his opportunity for an education; and destroy his whole future? Please don't be that kind of coach…and there are plenty of them

64

out there. You have the opportunity *and the obligation* to be better than that.

The main point is clear; you want your players to compete with every fiber of their beings, but there are certain lines you do not cross. You must teach them that this drive and determination does not extend to the point of deliberately injuring another player. Injuries are an inevitable part of sports, but players know the difference between a good, hard, clean shot on an opponent and a cheap shot. Always teach your players to compete *clean, fair, and legal*.

* * * * * *

Let's look at the positive side of competition. After all, that's what life is all about. When you're taking a test in school, you're trying to get the best score you can because, if the teacher grades on a curve, you want your score to be the one at the top. When you apply for a job, you're competing with all the other applicants. If you're a sales person, you're always competing for that sale and that commission, bonus, or maybe even a promotion associated with successful salesmanship.

I once had a very talented baseball team. Unfortunately, they lacked confidence. These players were very experienced, but somehow, their previous coaches were unsuccessful at getting these players to believe in themselves. Now, I don't want my players to be arrogant and cocky, but in order to do their best, they must be confidant that they can make the play that they are attempting.

I had spent enough time with these players to have a good handle on what they could and couldn't do. That is one thing that a coach must be able to do. You have to be able to recognize what a player can and cannot do. Do not put him in a position where he will fail. In other words, don't put the slowest player in the outfield position where he will have to cover a lot of ground. He simply can't do it. You can't put him there and then blame him for not making the plays. Put him where his assets will be best utilized and his weaknesses will be minimized.

I know this sounds easy but quit rolling your eyes. I've seen a high school basketball coach run an offense where his 6' 7" non-ballhandling center routinely received the ball at the top of the key. Needless to say, the opposing guards had a field day stealing the ball from him. The center wasn't equipped for this type of assignment. The coach blamed his player for losing the ball. He couldn't figure out that he had set the player up to fail with the offense he was running. Go ahead and say, "Well, duh!" (I did.) (Be sure to use plenty of sarcasm too.)

Back to my baseball team. These kids were eighth graders with a few young high school freshmen. We were in the middle of the season and were at the point where I had them in the correct positions, with back-ups and contingency plans in place. They just needed to believe in themselves and go out and make the play. They had to quit playing on their heels, hoping the ball would be hit some place else.

We're getting ready for a Sunday afternoon home game. There would be a good crowd and our opponent always brought a lot of people so it would be a terrific, competitive atmosphere. After warm-ups, I took the team out to right field so we could be isolated from prying ears.

I talked to them about their abilities and the progress they had made so far that season. I recounted specific plays in practices and games. I got all of the kids involved in the plays that I cited. I pointed out the difficulty of this play and that, and how each player that made the successful play needed to recognize how good it was and that a lesser player could not have done what he did.

I accelerated from there, pointing out some plausible game situations, getting them to imagine the ball being hit to them and making the play. I wanted them to want the ball hit to them in that critical situation. I was really building to a crescendo now.

In my best Baptist minister voice, I exhorted them to believe in themselves. "You've got to want every ball hit to you! You've got to know that you can make that play! You have to believe that you are the best player on this field!!!" (Practically shouting by now.)

Now, I picked the cockiest kid on the team. He was also very good, but it was his attitude that caused me to select him. By now, I am at a fever pitch and so are the kids. My plan is to call out each player and get his involvement and affirmation that he can – and wants to – make the play. To get this ball rolling like a snowball picking up steam, I chose this little spitfire first.

Shouting now, "Andy, who's the toughest son of a gun on this team?!?" Andy shouts back, "I am, Coach!" I immediately picked another kid, probably our smartest baseball player, an excellent fielder, but very quiet and unassuming. "Eric," I shout, "Who's the toughest son of a gun on this team?!?" Eric slowly raised his hand to point at the other player and quietly said, "Andy."

I was so into the moment, really in my element getting my players ready to play and Eric stuck a pin in my big ol' balloon of bravado. It was hard not to burst out laughing and I'm not sure that I didn't. (Looking back, it was actually hilarious, but at the time, well...) Needless to say, the pep talk was over. I tried to recover and get them back on track, but I definitely did not have the same fanfare.

Ironically, when I looked at the other dugout, the opposing coach was an acquaintance with whom I had played basketball for many years. He was the single most competitive individual I have ever met. How's that for a serious dose of irony?

As you might have guessed, this speech also went into the archives of the, "How Not To..." chapter. Looking back, had I chosen a different player second and established a rhythm of, "I am!" responses coming from each player, I think Eric might have fallen in line. I'm sorry to digress. Right now, I'm shaking my head at myself in disappointment but still laughing at the hilarity of the moment. I need to change the subject.

* * * * * *

I titled this chapter, "I know more than they do. This'll be easy." But there are times when I learned from my players. Always keep your mind open for new ideas, no matter if they come from another coach, a parent, or even from someone of the much smaller variety. Remember the old adage, "Out of the mouths of babes…"

My playing days were spent with the strictest of disciplinarian coaches. Back then, that was the norm and we didn't think anything of it. Today, some of those heavy-handed techniques that we endured would be frowned upon and might possibly be legally actionable. Without going into detail about coaches from another generation, suffice it to say that, as a player, I was subjected to many fire and brimstone speeches.

Because of this programming in my youth and the fact that I am very competitive, I tend to expect my players to have that same hard-nosed attitude. I want to see that fierce look in their eyes when I give them that certain motivational talk. You know the one. It's the one that builds to that fever pitch, where your players are ready to rip the locker room door off its hinges just to get at the other team.

I can see that many of you are nodding in the affirmative because that is exactly the type of player you want on your team. Well, let me tell you that there is an entirely different kind of personality that is also very productive and one that I would gladly have on my teams. But it took a very young player to teach me this lesson.

I met John, (not his real name), when I drafted his older brother as a receiver for a football team. In most leagues with which I am familiar, siblings go to the same team. Any way, little brother John fit in nicely. He was a good kid and I never had any problem with him.

One thing I noticed with John was that he didn't seem to have that fire in his eyes. I didn't think much of it since he was young and small. With football, it takes some kids some time to get used to the physical nature of the sport.

I know a man who was a superior athlete when he was in school so he played Cub (8th grade) football as a seventh grader. Cub football was run by the high schools and involved some beginning weight lifting and was much more physical than most youth leagues. As one of the youngest players on the team, he regularly played on the hamburger squad. In short, he got the snot kicked out of himself the entire season.

He went on to become a starting high school quarterback, leading his team to the state championship and earning All-State honors. He went to a Big Ten school on a scholarship as a quarterback. Even with the burden of playing big time Division I football, he was accepted to medical school and has been a doctor for many years.

We talked about his football career a few of years ago, well into adulthood. He told me how that first year of playing football in the seventh grade affected him. He said he never got used to that concussive sound of the plastic on plastic helmet crack when the bigger, older players hit him.

I imagine this probably made him a bit timid at first. He was probably unsure of himself during that first season. I bet he had a bit of a lackluster look in his eyes on more than one occasion. Not that fire and brimstone, piss and vinegar, "let me at 'em," kind of look. But he stuck to it and became a fantastic quarterback.

That conversation resonated with me as I thought about John. It was his second year with me when he became a defensive starter. He was a safety. He was smart, fast, had good hands, and could really track a ball. Needless to say, he got numerous interceptions and by midway through the season, the other teams would not throw to his side. One day, he complained to me that these other teams would not throw the ball his way. I immediately responded, "Great!"

That thoroughly confused him. I went into a detailed explanation of how that was a sign of respect that the other coaches had for his ability. He was simply too good for them so they quit trying to beat him with their passing game. He was still frustrated that he didn't get any action, so I found more places to use him.

This was a very good player and a great young man. He wasn't whining or complaining; he was just hungry to help the team more. Still, I didn't, "see," that toughness in him. When I gave him that, "toughen up, let's go punish the other team," speech, he looked more like a bobble head doll than a hard-nosed football player.

One day, I was watching film of one of our games. It was a close game so, at one point, we used an on-sides kick. It was executed perfectly, obviously because of my brilliant coaching, but also because it was at a time when the other team did not expect it. Oh yes, I should mention that we had really good players too. That always helps.

As the ball squibbed into a dead area behind our opponent's front line, our players were flying to the ball. One of their players got there first and was bending to pick up the ball. We all know that is a major no-no, but still we see it even in professional games. The correct play, of course, is to fall on the ball in a fetal position and hang on for dear life.

Since their player was the first one to get there, our first arrival could not get the ball so he did what he had been taught. He knocked their player out of the way and depended on his teammates to recover the ball, which they did. The hit was so quick that both players flew out of the camera view.

I rewound and re-watched that hit many times but all I saw was a yellow blur of a player as he wiped out the blue guy. (We were the Steelers; they were the Cowboys.) Finally, I resorted to asking my son to watch the film and tell me who made the hit. My son has extraordinary eyesight, the value of which is immeasurable in athletics. (Bald eagles routinely ask for his help in spotting distant field mice.) He could see quite clearly that it was indeed John who made that hit. As I've said, John always did his job, but I never saw him hit so fiercely. I was starting to learn of his toughness, but the best was yet to come.

Fast-forward a couple of years. The baseball team that he played on folded so he and several teammates came to join our team. John had grown a little bit but he was still very thin and without the shoulder pads, there was just not much to him. He was anything but physically imposing. Do not let that fool you about your players. Watch their deeds, not the size of the package.

It was the middle of July and the hottest day of the year. (Hey, I'm telling the story so if I want it to be the hottest day of the year, then it was.) The temperature was well into the 90s and with the river on which our town was built, the humidity regularly reached above 90% as it was on this day.

We were playing at our main rival's baseball field. They were always way better than we were so ordinarily the game shouldn't have been much of a contest. This season was a bit different. They were not as

73

good as usual and we were better than usual so the competition was a bit closer. And we had John.

We started him at pitcher and, due to the heat, we watched his pitch count very carefully. We made sure all of the players stayed hydrated. Still, by the end of the second inning, John was a major sweat ball.

After three innings, John had a low pitch count and we were ahead 3 – 0. He was getting stronger each inning. He felt fine and wanted to keep pitching. (Hmmm, competitive much?) I talked to his dad and asked him to watch John closely so if we missed any clues, his dad could pick up on them and we could pull John. Dear old dad assured me that John thrived on hot weather so he should be all right, but still, we had an extra set of eyes on him.

As each inning went by, John just got stronger. We had stretched the lead to 6 – 2 by the middle of the fifth and our opponent couldn't hit John very well at all. In the bottom half of the fifth, they got a runner to third base with one out. John threw a passed ball and immediately, players were sprinting for home plate.

Their runner was charging hard from third in an attempt to score. John was covering they plate as the catcher retrieved the ball. The catcher threw wide to the third base side of the plate. This caused John to dive to make the catch. As he did this, the base runner went into his slide.

The ball and both players arrived at the plate at the same time. As John dove for the ball, the runner slid right into John, kicking him hard right in the ribs. The soaking wet John (complete with his glasses) went rolling in the opposite direction and all you could see was a big cloud of dust. From somewhere in the middle of the dust cloud, you could distinctly hear John say rather matter-of-factly, "That's going to hurt in the morning," as he continued rolling to a halt.

The runner was safe. John got up and walked back to the mound. Notice I didn't say, "He dusted himself off?" There was no dusting him. He was mud covered. We wiped him off, checked his health, and got out of his way. He had a ball game to win. He did, 7 – 3, and he pitched a complete game.

That game and that play put the exclamation point on John's toughness. His dad was always very supportive, but he never interfered. It wasn't until we talked after the season about John's approach to athletics. His dad told me John was happy-go-lucky in everything he did. As long as he was loose, he was ready to do whatever was needed. This included schoolwork, the marching band, or his sports. If you tried to get John to burn white hot, well, that just wasn't his nature. He couldn't be nearly as effective that way as when he was loosey-goosey.

I hope you have many players like John. More importantly, I hope you recognize what lies beneath what I can only refer to as a slightly offbeat demeanor. If I would have tried to force John into my perception of a competitive warrior, both of us would have failed. Still, this was one tough bobble-head doll. By not pressuring John to fit my mold, he was able to perform much closer to his potential – and that's always your goal with any player. I learned the key for this player's performance from the player himself. Thank you, John.

Yes, you probably do know more about the sport you're coaching than your players do, but that's only part of it. First, don't assume they have already learned stuff. You have to be able to communicate your messages very clearly for *all* of the players. Remember too that they are not all George Patton clones. Some of them have that fire hidden beneath a rather thick veneer, but their method of utilizing it is no less valid than yours. You have to learn to reach all types of players because until you do, you can't tell who the best ones will be.

IV. Problem Child/Problem Parent

When you embark on the arduous task of the upcoming season, you naively may assume that everyone else is as positive and as eager to work together as you are. (Tsk, tsk, tsk, silly coach.) Not everyone shares your optimism. And not everyone is as wonderfully charming and easy to get along with as you are. Sometimes there is a bad apple hiding in that barrel of fun-loving kids awaiting your valued instruction. It may be a parent or it may be a child, or guess what. It may be both and there's a good chance they will be related.

First, let's explore the tricky little world of dealing with a problem parent. We all know, but it certainly bears repeating that not all people are alike, at any age. You will run into value systems much different than yours. I have erred already by assuming there actually *is* a value system in place within the homes of all of these youngsters. Sadly, you may find that some children are like a rudderless dinghy afloat in the great big sea we refer to as life. You may be the only steadying influence that some of these children encounter on a day-to-day basis. Surprisingly, sometimes these children are easier to work with than those children

77

whose parents are heavily involved in their lives...*too* heavily involved. (You know: helicopter parents.)

It may shock you to learn that, although your way of looking at the world is certainly the fairest, most objective viewpoint ever to be so carefully formulated, others may not always share your wisdom. And there's the rub. Different parents will instill in their children all sorts of concepts, loosely having to do with what is right and what is wrong. This is where you have to tippy-toe ever so gently across the minefield that is your team's collective psyche. You must establish the rules for the team, the guidelines for behavior and strike the balance whereby you treat all children equivalently, while respecting their individuality, while still insisting on adherence to team rules, thereby promoting team unity.

Any time you are involved with someone else's child, you are going to be met with varying degrees of skepticism. Some people will greet you and the upcoming season with as much unbridled optimism as their children. (You want to clone those people because they are the ones that will make your job easier.) Others will give you the benefit of the doubt as long as Little Johnny is playing and is happy. Every now and again, you will have the misfortune to have a parent who has a chip on his or her shoulder and, try as you might, you and your league can't do anything good enough for Little Johnny.

Understand that parents like these have a preconceived notion of your obvious inferiority. Add to this mindset the fact that they have never seen what goes on in your little corner of the coaching world. And oh, by the way, they have never been involved except for the part where they feel the need to point out your incompetence. Hmmm,…and their expertise comes from where?

I was a part (well, a bystanding part) of a great solution to just such a problem. This was in my first year of coaching and it was football. I was assisting a 24 year old kid who, in addition to his vast football knowledge was also very adept at handling people. I found out later that he worked in the HR department of a major manufacturer where he had lots of experiencing handling grown-up children if you know what I mean.

For you to get the full effect of this story – and we all want that, don't we – I must first give you a complete mental picture of the player involved in this problematic situation.

Bobby was a six year old playing on a team for seven, eight, and nine year olds. Believe it or not, some six year olds are ready, but most lack the emotional maturity to focus - squirrel – for any length of time. He spent most of his time at practices rolling around in the grass playing with the practice dummies. O. k., that seemed redundant even as I wrote it.

We had difficulty getting any effort whatsoever out of little Bobby. His mother attended every practice, as did many parents. I don't know if she had her nose buried in a book or just thought of this as an *al fresco* baby-sitting service or what. Regardless, It soon became clear that she did not communicate the news of Bobby's participation, or lack thereof, to her husband.

When the players ran a conditioning lap around the green trash can at the far end of the practice facility, it was all we could do to get Bobby to return. His pace was not that of a jog, nor a spirited walk even. It was more reminiscent of a turtle, if the specific turtle used for this analogy tended to meander with no sense of urgency to complete his assigned route.

Tackling drills for Bobby consisted of avoiding contact if he were the 'tacklee.' If he were the tackler, he made an effort that would convince any self-respecting father to enroll him in something far less physical and *al fresco*, like maybe an indoor tiddly winks league.

Needless to say, little Bobby didn't see much playing time. Oh, we had other players who were basically inept at football. This certainly is understandable because very few of these kids had any previous exposure to football other than two or three neighbor kids running around tackling each other. The difference with Bobby was that he gave no effort. Really, there wasn't much we could do with little Bobby at this point in the season…or at this stage of his life.

It was several games into the season when little Bobby's dad was able to attend his first game. As I mentioned, apparently little Bobby's mom hadn't provided progress reports to the dad. This game was business as usual. Little Bobby played a very minimal amount. On this day, he was right along the sidelines with all the other players, almost attentive you might say. (I said, "*almost.*")

Well, after the game, little Bobby's dad asked to speak with us coaches. We gladly obliged. Then it happened. He went ballistic. He couldn't believe little Bobby wasn't the star around whom the entire league was formed. He ranted and raved at what seemed like an eternity but I'm sure it was only a minute or so.

The head coach looked him right in the eye very attentively and nodded his head in agreement during the entire rant. This took the wind out of angry dad's sails so he gave the coach a chance to respond. The coach, this young kid (remember he's only 24) very enthusiastically asked for his help. He quickly and passionately explained that there were only the two of us and we could surely use his help.

You should have seen angry dad perk up and change his entire approach to the situation. Now, the coach made it seem as if we just couldn't get along without him. He was the key to our chance for a successful season. He explained that he was on a swing shift rotation and that, although he couldn't make every practice, the following week he would be able to make it.

One practice was all it took. This dad got a first hand look at little Bobby rolling around with the tackling dummies. He watched with wondering eyes as little Bobby dodged tackle after tackle. When the players ran their first conditioning lap, I thought he was going to burst a blood vessel as he exploded at little Bobby to hustle. It did no good. Little Bobby was nowhere close to being ready for football at this age, but as a teaching tool, his dad made him finish the season.

Ballistic dad apologized to us after that first practice. He explained that with his rotating shift, he had not slept for 36 hours prior to his outburst at the previous Saturday's game. He understood what we had gone through and told us he would address it with little Bobby. He would leave the coaching to us.

I don't know what went on at home, but Bobby came back for the next practice with an entirely different attitude. He began to give some effort and contributed what he could. One practice, after one of the older players delivered a nice hard block on him during a kickoff return, Bobby got up ripping and snorting. He asked if we could kick it again and this time, right to the offending player because he wanted a chance to tackle him and get even. Fantastic! What a great change of attitude! (Not that he stood a snowball's chance of accomplishing that feat, but still…)

Bobby's progress was a bonus that we hadn't expected. The real message here is how to handle an angry parent. This was kind of the perfect storm for this tactic because the head coach knew that once the dad got a good look at Bobby's practice habits, he would get the message. It was the coach's enthusiastic approach to embracing the angry parent that worked magic. What a sales job!...or was it a snow job? Anyway, as the saying goes, "You catch more flies with honey than you do with vinegar."

I have been very fortunate in my career that I have not been confronted by many disgruntled parents. The key to this is simply keeping them informed of anything that may affect them throughout the season. I always invited them to ask questions if they had any…and then just prayed that they wouldn't have any. I don't care for talking with parents during a season because they don't listen as well as their kids do – and we are quite aware how well kids listen to adults who are giving instructions. Also, parents assume they know way more than they actually do. Still, the key is good communication from beginning to end.

Be The
Ultimate
Sports Coach

V. Go Stand on the Block

Coaches at the earliest stages of a player's development are focused on teaching the basics of the sport...or at least they should be. Very young players have not even learned the fundamentals necessary to participate in the sport. That needs to be the coach's focus. You also want to teach the basic rules of the game, and as an extension of that, teach them to compete, "Clean, fair, and legal."

No matter what age you are coaching, techniques & fundamentals, rules, and fierce but fair competition should always be your focus. I think we can all agree that I am the master of stating the obvious, right? *Then why don't coaches do these things?*

Seriously folks, I have watched high school senior basketball players who couldn't shoot a basketball properly. I'm not talking about making baskets. I'm talking about not knowing and using the proper technique. How does that happen? Coaches get too wrapped up in their own agendas and forget that one of the synonyms for the word, "coach," is "teach." You should be there to actually *teach* your players, not just make sure they run through specific drills each day.

84

Let's get back to that example of the high school senior basketball player with the terrible shooting form. I once coached just such a player. His form wasn't some deviation of the basic shooting form. It was so bad; it was as if the boy had never seen another person shoot a ball in his life. How could he get to high school in his senior season without knowing proper shooting technique? There are a number of plausible answers to that question, most having to do with a lack of quality coaching throughout his youth. One thing I could tell immediately about this kid was that he was very intelligent and very coachable.

I taught him how to shoot properly in a very short time. It did not take him long to improve to the point where he once hit four three-point shots in one game…and this kid was not blessed with an overabundance of basketball talent. Still, he was very smart and very coachable so this shooting fix was relatively simple.

I have watched many practices of players of all ages in different sports and in the vast majority of them; coaches spent no time teaching proper techniques. When you see players whose fundamentals are behind where they should be for their age, you know they have not had good coaching.

When is the easiest time to teach proper technique? Of course, the younger the better. (i. e., Son, as soon as I change your diaper, you hit two free throws on your Little Tykes Basketball Goal; then it's bed time.)

As players age and pass from one coach to the other, this lack of exposure to the fundamentals often continues. If none of the player's coaches teach the fundamentals, the player will only learn by watching and guessing. That's how kids get to high school and have yet to learn the proper techniques to enable them to execute whatever the coaches are asking of them. Too many players get bigger, faster, and stronger as a function of the aging process but they don't get better skill-wise.

Why does this happen? One reason is that coaches are always under a time constraint. Have you ever heard a coach say he has too much practice time? Coaches look at the date of that first game and start implementing offenses and defenses. Never mind that the players have awful fundamentals. The coach still places all of his emphasis on getting the team to *appear* ready to play that first game. Do yourself and your players a favor by taking the time to teach basic techniques. That may mean spending extra time before or after practice with certain players on specific skills.

As players progress in their skill level and their understanding of the basics of the game(s), they are beginning to develop the one thing that is their biggest asset for playing the sport. This is another area of a player's development that coaches often neglect and sometimes negate.

What is it you ask? (Thanks for playing along.) This is how I teach my players this very lesson.

I always ask my teams what each player's most valuable asset is – or I ask them to name the best thing that a player brings to the field (or court). I single out players as examples and ask the team to name his best asset. Picking distinctly different players one by one always confuses the kids. The answer is the same for every player, but rather than tell them, I want to make them think and arrive at the correct answer.

Naturally, when you pick your biggest football player and ask what the best thing is about him, his teammates begin guessing size, strength, his mom is a good cook, etc. Without giving them the answer, switch to your small speedster and ask the same question. By now, you'll definitely see confused looks. When you give them a third player, give them a hint. (You can only get so much enjoyment out of tormenting children. *I'm kidding.*)

My hint was always the same. I told them the answer is the same for all players. That always sparked more confused looks and odd guesses. The next hint was that it's what's above their shoulders. By that point, they guess it correctly. It's their brains, their minds. A player in any sport can't do the right thing until he knows what the right thing is. I don't want any empty helmets running around on my teams. I have always preferred coaching a smart player to the alternative. Now, here's the shocker. *All of those helmets are empty until a coach fills them.*

The more inexperienced a player is at a sport – regardless of age, the more his head is like that of an infant. There is a certain level of ability to understand and learn new things, but until somebody exposes them to this new information, that little sponge-like brain will have nothing to absorb. The players need (and deserve) good information.

Think about it. If so many coaches are willing to skip teaching the proper fundamental skills so they can get to their complex offenses and defenses, do you really think they are going to spend a lot of time teaching their players how to think their way through certain game situations? They aren't.

Can you imagine how difficult it would be to think of every possible surprise a player could see during the course of a playing career and explain exactly how to handle the situation? It's impossible. Yet too many coaches spend their time telling players exactly what to do on a given play. (That play that was drawn beautifully on the chalkboard…but seldom – if ever – is run to perfection during actual competition.)

My coaching philosophy is quite different from these types of coaches. I believe in teaching players how to think their way through the game, not just do what they're told. Don't get me wrong; I believe in a lot of structure. I won't allow my players to run around willy-nilly; although sometimes it's hard to differentiate their best efforts from that willy-nilly thing.

As far as the structure goes, everyone on my teams has a very clear choice. Learn their plays and their assignments and they will play or don't learn them and sit on the bench. Their playing time is not my decision. It's theirs. This is another way of getting players to take ownership of their playing time and the direction of the team.

There is an awful lot more to every sport beyond what any coach can draw on a chalkboard and you want your players to be prepared to handle any situation that might arise during a game. This might upset a lot of coaches but by controlling their players, they are limiting the scope of the players' learning. Coaches are also limiting the quality and success of their teams by strictly controlling their players. I want my players to run their plays perfectly, but I don't want them looking at me all confused when something doesn't go according to what I've drawn on the board. I don't want my player to panic if he is supposed to go stand on the block, but when he gets there, an opponent is already standing on the block, thereby making it impossible for him to complete his assignment. I want him to *figure it out!!!*

Remember that play that was drawn so perfectly on the blackboard? I've got news for you; that isn't the way games are played. No coach can tell his players exactly where the opponents are going to be or how they will react to certain situations. That is why your players have to be prepared for the unexpected. You have to give the players all of the

89

information about what the play is to accomplish and what each segment of the play is designed to accomplish.

The player's job is not to go and stand exactly on the block. He is either screening a player in that area; receiving a pass in that area; or maybe getting position for an entry pass or rebound. Whatever the mission, that opponent standing on the block may be part of your player's assignment; he's just standing a few feet off from the spot where the coach said he'd be. The player needs to be able to adjust to this slight variation and execute the play properly. That's what successful players do.

******

I once watched a high school team's pre-season intra-squad football scrimmages. The freshmen played the JV team and the varsity first team played the varsity second team. In the freshman vs. JV game, the freshmen had the ball at midfield. The quarterback dropped back to pass, saw that his primary receiver was covered, and checked down to another receiver. He put his pass right on the money and his receiver caught it at the five yard line. Good play, right? We'll see.

90

I noticed the coach talking to the quarterback after that play. Not long after the game, I had an opportunity to talk with the quarterback. I asked what the coach said after that play. He said the coach was mad. He had told the QB to throw to the right side wide out who ran a chair route. That's where the receiver goes up field ten yards, cuts right to the sideline, then cuts left and runs straight up the side line.

As you can imagine, this is a very slow developing route for most high school players to run. The receiver was double covered. The quarterback opted not to throw a long - i. e., low percentage – pass into double coverage. Instead, he found a wide open receiver inside the ten yard line. Seems like a good idea, right? Not for that coach. It was more important to him that players did exactly as they were told. Definitely in the, *"what to avoid!"* category.

I understand that players are supposed to run the plays that the coach tells them to, but ultimately it is the player's responsibility to make a good play. If he throws the long pass into double coverage, it is very unlikely that anything good will come of it. The quarterback did what any good quarterback should do. He found an open receiver, made a good play, and put his team at the five yard line. The most important factor in the making of this good play was that the quarterback first had to make a good decision.

On another occasion a year later, I watched this same quarterback play in a JV game. From the opponents' 30 yard line, he ran a play action fake to the fullback, then spun and threw a perfect touchdown pass to the tight end at the goal line. As the QB came off the field, this same coach came to talk with him.

You guessed it. The quarterback screwed up again. What an idiot quarterback. He was supposed to throw to a very slow receiver who was double covered in the left flat. The quarterback said both wide receivers were doubled covered with the safeties providing the extra coverage. That left the middle of the field with no defenders. He knew the tight end on the right side was running a fly pattern to that wide open pasture so why not throw it to him for an easy touchdown? That's exactly what the quarterback did. Silly quarterback. By not doing exactly what the coach said, he had made a bad decision. Same coach once again illustrating *what to avoid!*

You might think that as the coach in a situation like this, you know more about the game of football than your high school quarterback does. That coach certainly thought so. (He was wrong but that's a different discussion for a different day.)

If you teach your players to do exactly *and only* what you tell them, they will not have the ability to think of what to do when the unexpected happens. Well, unexpected things do happen and players need to know how to deal with these curveballs. Guess what; I don't care if I don't get credit for the good plays my players make. I just want them to make them. I want them to learn how to figure out what to do in the heat of the moment. After all, it's their responsibility to make a good play. Do you think it's better to teach your players to obey your every word or to learn how to think their way through the game?

As I once told that coach, it doesn't matter what you draw on the chalkboard. Once the ball is snapped, your planning can go right out the window. You might have a grand design on where each defender will be and what each defender will do, but that doesn't always happen. The flaw in this coach's thinking was that he did not realize that being on the sideline, he couldn't see what the quarterback saw. Wouldn't it be a good thing to teach the quarterback how to think the game instead of always doing exactly what the coach told him to do?

The fact is the quarterback sees the field more clearly than the coach on the sidelines and once the ball is snapped, the QB is the only person who is in position to read the defense and have an impact on the play. Since the quarterback is the one person who is in the best position to assess the situation on the field, doesn't it make sense to teach him how to do so? After all, regardless of what happens, it's the quarterback's (and every player's) responsibility to make a good play: the right play for the situation. Sometimes, that's different than what the coach thinks prior to the snap of the ball. This coach was teaching obedience, not football.

So, by all means, spend your time and effort teaching your players to understand the game. When players can think, make the right decisions, and ultimately execute a good play, doesn't that make the coach look good? Of course it does, but some coaches' egos get in the way and they feel they must control every aspect of every play. Once again: *what to avoid!*

It might sound simple to teach players how to intuitively think their way through the various game situations they will encounter. That is not the case but, like most coaches, I did not understand how to teach this concept at first. There is a fine line between teaching players how to execute the play as it was diagrammed vs. how to understand the objective of the play and how to accomplish that objective when the defense has thrown a monkey wrench into the mix.

******

I figured this out when I tried to teach a basketball offense I learned when I was in high school. To get your players to understand every nuance of your scheme, be ready to fully explain your offense, defense, etc. I know; this sounds obvious. But until you've been on both sides of this fence, you won't realize the difference between how a player perceives an offense and how a coach sees an offense.

94

When I was in high school, I learned an offense that my high school coach had been running for years. It is called the Shuffle. I didn't know the history of it then, but as a high school running that offense, we were ahead of our time. It is categorized as a, "continuity offense," which is a term I never heard until much later in life.

In high school, I learned all the basic cuts and passes. One passes to two; five screens for three; and then goes down to the block to screen for four, etc. I learned how, at the end of the first round of cuts in the offense, the players have moved through their rotations so that the offense was set up the same on the other side of the court. Specific players were not in the same positions from which they started but each spot was occupied and the same patterns could be run from the opposite side of the court. That's all I learned.

When I taught that offense for the first time, it was as if the heavens opened up, the lights came on, and I could see the big picture. In this particular offense, for every cut, there is a built-in back cut. The offense is designed to function when the defense plays in any positions. If the defense plays over the top for instance, or denies a specific pass, players can always use back door cuts. The entire offense is based on the ability to properly read and set screens.

In basketball, reading and setting screens are two of the most important skills that players need in order to be successful. These skills are used in every offense, no matter if it is a set offense, motion offense, continuity offense, or whatever. If they can learn these skills, they can execute any offense that any coach wants to teach.

The thing is, when teaching the Shuffle; I began with the basic positions. (Wing, elbow, block, point…) Then, the real teaching began. I explained the purpose of the offense and what outcome(s) we wanted to achieve. You can kinda play, "What if," with the players and get them to think and visualize what they would do in specific situations.

The defender is supposed to be here, but what if he isn't? What if he plays it this way? Show your players what to do in all of the possible variations the defenders can throw at them. The offensive player has to be able to read the defender's position, and then cut accordingly, i. e., over the top, back door, flair, etc. If you restrict your players to just doing exactly what you say, they will never learn how to make good adjustments when the opposing players don't stand exactly where you drew the little "X"s on your chalkboard.

Remember, game knowledge that may appear intuitive in an advanced player had to be learned somewhere along the way. If you don't teach players all of these subtleties, you can't yell at them for not knowing these nuances. They may have had bad coaching before they got to you so no matter what their ages, you can't assume they already know a whole bunch of this stuff.

The major point of this whole chapter can be summed up in one sentence. Don't just tell a player to go stand on the block; teach him *why* he is going to stand on the block. Teach him what to do if that block is already occupied. Now you've got a player who can think the game, not just do what you tell him to do. If you teach your players to think the game, you are getting them closer to reaching their potential. Isn't that the goal?

VI. Don't Set Goals; Establish Your Level of Expectation
OR
Don't Set Goals; Set the Bar of Excellence
OR
Don't Set Goals; Establish (Your) Standards

Obviously, to succeed at anything, you need to set goals so that's kind of a stupid chapter title, right? Stick with me here. You will always have goals for yourself and you will always have goals for your players, but here's the key. There is a subtle difference, but an important one, between setting goals and establishing standards.

Actually, establishing your standards is the first thing you do. Parents are expected to attend that first practice. Players are expected to be at all practices on time. Players are expected to have all of their equipment at every practice. Players are expected to follow your coaching rules. All of these things are non-negotiable. These are not goals; they are your standards. After that comes setting goals.

The next step is establishing your standards of excellence with regard to performance. Your players are there to *learn* the sport so you can't expect them to be perfect at anything on the first day. (Well, duh!)

When you teach a specific skill, I have found it best to describe the technique and explain it piece by piece. Tell the players why each

98

step is significant and why it must be done that way. If there is something that can be done in different ways, don't insist on everyone doing it *just..one..way*. Players' bodies are designed differently and what may be easy for one kid may not be easy for another simply due to physical limitations.

Take for example, shooting a basketball. The absolute perfect, textbook method of shooting has both elbows in, roughly in line with your shoulders. You don't want the elbows pointed outward because it can do goofy things to your shot. Guess what. Some people's joints are just a bit different. They can't put their elbows in line with their shoulders without that causing their wrists to turn at an angle.

If you're trying to shoot a basketball straight ahead, you don't want your wrist turned inward. Turn the shooting hand's wrist so it's straight and guess what? That elbow may go out of your textbook position. You'll need to keep the basics of what you are teaching, but there are variations that are within an acceptable range. In the case of shooting a basketball, the release is far more important than anything else. You need to be flexible in teaching those fundamentals.

To continue the example of shooting a basketball, when teaching each player a comfortable shooting motion, avoid bringing up a specific player; college, pro, or whatever. You can end up debating shooting techniques of different players 'til the cows come home. The same applies to any sport you may be coaching. Invariably, your player will come up with some player who has the most unorthodox shooting style, but may still be a good shooter. He'll try to justify his own screwy shot technique based on this one-in-a-million exception to the rule. It's tough to convince a young player that he does not have the same physical talent that his chosen professional athlete has. That's not the point here anyway so don't digress and don't let your players derail you in your message. (Like I just did getting into shooting performances.)

Nearly everything you teach, no matter what sport, will follow this model. The main thing is to get the core components the same with each kid. This is especially true with things that can cause injury if not done properly. Take tackling in football for example.

Once you have explained, *in detail*, how to perform a proper tackle, demonstrate it in slow motion and stop action. Show each step and stop to be sure each player can see the technique as you progress through the steps. Of all the sports I've coached, this is the single most important thing to get perfect because, potentially it can be the most injurious.

I was fortunate when I taught tackling to my youth teams. I had two of the best form tacklers you'd ever want to see tackle on my football teams for six years. Maybe it was because they were small that they understood the importance of proper tackling if they were to get the job done. They learned proper technique the first year I taught them. After that, they just got better.

Both of them had perfect form. Both were very strong, intense hitters. For the purposes of, "Setting the Bar of Excellence," the best thing about them was, they were two of the smallest players on any team on which they played. Why is that good, you ask? Thank you for asking. This is where we segue into setting the standards for the players.

I must admit that I stumbled upon this technique quite by accident. It was my first year as a head football coach. We had been through the required non-contact days and were ready to start full contact drills. For my teams, that meant learning to tackle.

We had already gone through the step-by-step instructions on proper tackling technique. The first thing I did with fully padded players was to explain once again every single step to the tackling process. When you have a basic function that is this important to the game and to the health of the players, you need to spend the extra time to be sure they get it right. Leave nothing to chance.

I assigned the players partners based on size and perceived ability. With the veterans, I knew who would make good match-ups; with the new players, I did the best I could. If you get a mismatch, you can always make changes. We did a few walk-throughs and the coaches looked at each pair of players individually.

By now, the players are getting antsy. They want to hit. The veterans are practically salivating – foaming at the mouth. This is when I created two lines of players, so the pairs were in the same position in

101

each line. My two mighty mites were first, one in each line. I finished lining the players up from next best to the weakest of the veterans. The rookies were paired up and went after all of the veterans.

I positioned the lines of players facing each other about five yards apart. They acted as the boundaries. The two players participating in the drill would be inside the gauntlet of the other players about five yards apart. A coach with a ball would be in the middle of each line of players.

The first few times through the rotation, one coach threw the ball the same direction every time so every player got the opportunity to run and to tackle. The next step was to have the coaches randomly alternate which one would throw the ball to either player. This way, the players had to be prepared for the ball to come from either direction and to either be the runner or the tackler.

Now, to the first hit. You've got all of these players anxious to get in on the action. For many of them, this was their first full contact football. With older teams, the principle is the same. The ones who are new to the team might think they are strong hitters, but the mighty mites set the bar of excellence for all of them. That's why I had them go first.

When I threw the first ball to one of the first pair, they went at each other in a way that would make any coach proud. It's about to bring a tear to my eye just thinking about it. They hit hard, with proper technique, and the tackle was made. They each popped right up, often helping each other up or slapping helmets or rear ends – you know how guys show respect. Remember, these guys were very small, yet their performance was outstanding.

Every player watching this knew that they had just seen what was expected. There was no, 'Well maybe this is sort of what it might be like...' It was now set in stone. This was the standard of this team. Don't forget, they were among the smallest players on the team. Actually, they were among the smallest in the entire league and yet they hit very hard – and with excellent technique. That made an impression on the rookies.

With each successive pair of veterans, the rookies got closer to their turns. The anticipation was palpable. The enthusiasm was there and I did not have to say anything to get their best efforts out of them because the mighty mites had shown them what was expected. The rookies had seen the standard for this team.

My teams were always the best tacklers in the league and it was largely due to that first hit by two small, ordinary looking kids. If you use big, strong kids, the little ones can use the size difference as an excuse for why they don't perform very well. Using the mighty mites showed that performing at that level can be done no matter how big or small you are.

I just got lucky having my two best form tacklers be so small. That gave me the opportunity to set up my tackling demonstrations as described above. That size thing just added to the impact they had on the rookies. Regardless of your situation or sport, the message is still the same. You are setting the standards to which all of your players must aspire. It is much easier for players to *see* your standards in their teammates than it is for them to hear you preach about it. Give them tangible demonstrations. My tackling aficionados had a much greater impact without me ever saying a word about how good they were.

******

While we're on happy accidents, I should relate a technique that I have adopted and used for many years. It is one of the core principles of my coaching philosophy. The situation that spawned this technique occurred during a football game but you will see how easily you can change it to fit any sport and any situation.

I had a very good team, but not the championship caliber team of some years. We had a very good fullback – the best in the league. He had played for me for several years. This was his second year as my fullback. He was not the fastest player around, but he was very strong and hit hard.

As a fullback, he was the lead blocker on many plays, especially on sweeps. When leading a sweep, there may be any number of players coming from different areas. I taught him to look for the toughest player, at the point of attack, who was in a position to make the tackle. I told him not to waste himself on one of the little guys who wasn't as likely to make the play. One of the other running backs or the ball carrier himself could handle the small fries.

I explained to him how he could tell where the ball carrier is by the actions of the defensive players. (Remember, the ball carrier is always behind him.) When leading the play, he was to scan the other players. He could tell by their eyes and how they moved where the ball carrier was and which way he was moving. From that quick assessment, he would be able to decide the best place for his block.

Beyond that, he would just have to practice. I assured him that he would make the wrong decision a bunch of times until he got the hang of it. How's that for being a good, supportive coach? It didn't take long for him to catch on to the nuances of his job.

You've heard that some players have, "…a nose for the ball." Well, this kid had a nose for the block. He had a natural talent for evaluating the opponents, their positions, the location of the football behind him, and choosing the right player to block. His blocks removed the best defender from the play and often times, put him on the ground.

We, as a team, got spoiled by our fullback's knack for blocking the right guy. On one particular instance, we faced a third down and seven at our opponents' thirty-five yard line. (Four down territory.) We ran a sweep left toward our sideline. As the play developed, everybody was in the proper position. The spacing was good. The fullback turned up field toward the approaching defenders. He chose his target, loaded up for the hit, and whiffed. Yep. Whiffed.

Just like Casey At The Bat. The stage was set. All he had to do was perform like he had for two seasons. We had seen him do it so well so many times; it wasn't a question of picking up the first down. The question was how many total yards we would gain on the play. And then it happened. The whiff. *He missed his block.*

The back got nailed for a five yard loss bringing up a fourth and twelve. As luck would have it, the fullback went face down in the dirt right at my feet. Still shocked by the missed block, I helped him up and I could see the dejected look on his face.

Now let me tell you that this young man, for all of his talent and all of the great plays he had made over the years, was not very confident. He was far more likely to get down on himself about the one play that he missed than he was to celebrate all of the others that he executed perfectly.

Remember too that I was a very excitable, demonstrative coach. I was always shouting, but in a positive manner. I want to make that distinction. Yes, I was a yeller and a screamer, but I did not yell *"at"* the players. I yelled in support of them. I always told them that they would never have a bigger cheerleader than me – except for maybe their parents and grandparents.

As I picked this fullback up from the ground, I was talking very loudly to snap him out of his pouty funk about missing the block. I had to get him to pay attention to my words. What came out of my mouth hit all of his hot buttons and I have used this technique for many years.

I told him in a very matter of fact manner, (And this was at a healthy shout while holding him by his shoulder pads) "Hey, you missed your block. Big deal. (I said that sarcastically.) That wasn't up to your level of play, but don't worry about it. You'll go out and hit the next ten in a row perfectly. You've done it before. Now, forget about that one and hit the next one like you know you can. Go tell the quarterback to run the same play to the other side. Hit your block and we'll pick up the first down."*

This was one frantic moment at the end of a play while the other players were returning to the huddle. I didn't have time to think about it or plan it. I saw a very upset kid who had just screwed up and possibly cost us a possession. What happened next could have made it worse for him but I didn't have time to script it; something just came out of my mouth and luckily for me, it wasn't stupidity.

I went back to standards. Not ours. *His*. His standard was that he always successfully led our sweeps. He always hit the hardest block on the best player on the other team. That was his standard of excellence. I simply reminded him, in the heat of the battle, and in a very loud, animated but positive manner that he was capable of playing at that standard, which he had set for himself. I also gave him his confidence back by having the team run the same play again and putting the fate of that possession in his hands.

******

It was after that season that I began talking to my teams more about playing to their potential without regard for the other team. O. k., I got a little lucky in football because I knew we had the best team that next season. If we played to the best of our ability, we would win. Hey, can't I stack the deck in my own favor in this psychological game of motivation with my team?

During one of the early preseason talks with a team, I will talk about our approach for the first game. I stipulate that veterans keep their mouths shut (because they already know the answer) and I ask the players if they know who our opponent is the first week. I do this a week and a half or so before that game so chances are the players don't have the schedule memorized.

Naturally the players start guessing. I always answer no. They guess so often that they begin duplicating their guesses. Finally I give them this hint: "It's the same as our opponent the second week." Confused looks, but still a few guesses. Then I continue; it's the same opponent as the next week and the next week and the next. By now, at least one of them will figure it out. The opponent is us, or rather the limits of our own potential.

Do not think the light bulb will go on for all of them. Not all of your players will progress from point "A" to point "B" to point "C" in logical fashion. Take the time to explain to them that we can't control what the other team does. We can only control what we do. If we constantly strive to be the best that we can be every play every day, we will continue to get closer to our potential. That's our goal.

We are always playing against our own potential. Think about it logically. You can't ask a player to be better than his potential. The best a player can do is the best he can do. How do you maximize that potential? You get better every play every day. That is one of my slogans, "Every play, every day."

If you give your best effort on every play every day in practice, that's all you can do. That's all you can ask of your players. If they do that, you are successful. Don't get me wrong. You still coach to win the games but sometimes, no matter how hard the players try; they may not have what it takes to defeat a far superior opponent. Still, your job is to push your players to the best of their potential.

You will be far more successful as a coach if you establish the attitude among your players of working toward their potential. When they quit worrying about other players on other teams and focus on performing their absolute best, you've got half of the battle won. Of course, somebody has to worry about the other team(s). That's your job! Why do you think they give you that big wheelbarrow full of money for doing this?

*The fullback did hit his block. We did get the first down. We did win the game. He continued to get better and excel at everything we asked of him. (I knew you'd want to know.)

VII. Developing That Winning Attitude

Shaping a player's attitudes for competition is an extremely important part of a player's development. It might sound obvious, but They have to learn the proper attitude someplace. If you look at some of the attitudes of people in today's world, you wonder how in the heck they got that way. Well, I'm here to blame their youth league athletic coaches! No, not really. I just like to joke around with you, the reader.

From sports, a participant should learn how to compete hard but fair, (remember clean, fair, and legal); to push themselves to the best of their potential; to be a good winner; and to be a good loser. No, I am not saying you should enjoy losing, but for all but the few players who become professionals, the sport in which they are competing is nothing more than a *game* but more importantly, it is an analogy for life.

For example, as an adult, when you find out that your competitor got the sales contract with your prospective client, i.e., you lost; do you kick the trash can across the room and throw a tantrum right there in the office? Look at the way some athletes behave when they lose a game, or even when a single call goes against them. I'm sure you've seen some examples of rather poor behavior.

If players were given a more complete education on what goes into participating in sports, they would be better prepared for successes and failures as they grow older. Notice I used the phrase, "grow older," because 'grow up' and 'mature' don't apply to the male of the species. We don't grow up as much as we just get a little older each year. We're still just bigger versions of little boys.

But seriously folks, you can really help your players by setting your rules and standing by your rules no matter how talented a specific player might be. The kids might not agree or understand it at the time, but when they mature a little, they will thank you for it. They might even actually understand why you did that dastardly deed that you did, whatever that may have been.

The lessons you teach can be large or small. I once had occasion to try and rein in control of a football practice but I tried to do it in the simplest and least disruptive way. The infraction wasn't a huge deal, but the player definitely was being counterproductive.

We had a very good veteran team. During one particular practice, one player – we'll call him Alex – (and you guessed it: not his real name) was not at all focused on the tasks at hand. Now, understand that Alex was not a particularly gifted athlete.

He was built reasonably strong, almost like a fullback type of running back, but he lacked the speed, balance, footwork, and well, talent necessary to be a running back. He was not "big enough" to be a lineman but he was not quick enough to be a running back. I guess you could say he was a 'tweener.'

Through his focus, hard work, and experience – this was his fifth year with me; he had become a valuable asset. He was a starter at right end. That was our power side so he was a good lead blocker for our power sweeps. He also had earned the number one back-up role for every other offensive line position. He was the first back-up defensive end as well as the back-up for any defensive line position. He was the equivalent of baseball's utility man. He was like having a wild card player, but on this day he was acting more like a joker. (I know you just love my plays on words.)

We were trying to run through some plays. We were going live so there was plenty of contact but nothing out of the ordinary. After every play, Alex was screwing around or messing with somebody. For a kid who got to where he was with his concentration and effort, this behavior was an aberration.

After one particular play, I had had enough of his antics. Rather than to dress him down in front of the whole team, I stopped practice just long enough to yell at Alex to, "Run down to that green trash can and come back and tell me what color it is!" (The reader might infer that, indeed there was a green trash can at the far end of the practice facility about 150 yards away.)

As Alex ran off to do his penance, the rest of the team cracked up laughing. I was utterly bewildered. I looked at my assistant coach. He looked mildly amused, probably stifling a hearty laugh because he was a bit more respectful of me and my fancy title of, "Head Coach," than the players. Still, I had no clue what was so funny.

I asked what was so funny and I was informed that I had specified that the trash can was in fact green, but Alex's assignment was nevertheless to inspect said trash can and report back to me to verify that yes, I was correct. The trash can was green. In my haste and frustration, I had no idea what I actually said. Actually, my blunder took the edge off of the situation.

Although I was so beside myself that I didn't realize what I had said, the strategy was firmly in place. Maintain the discipline of the team. Punish the offending player, but do not unnecessarily humiliate him. Don't get me wrong; I am not against yelling at a player. I mean, isn't yelling at other people's children one of the fun things about coaching? I'm just kidding. Please don't call the Department of Child Services.

Remember, you still want the 90% good contributions that he was capable of delivering. You want to remove his distractive behavior from the other players before they also become infected with this minor attack of goofiness. Don't forget, we're dealing with the male of the species and when one player gets goofy, it is only a matter of time before it spreads. (This tendency holds true for adult males as well.) Anyway, Alex's now legendary trip to the green trash can served the purpose. When he got back, he was much more focused on the task at hand. Remember, a tired puppy is always easier to train.

******

Another incident that proved to be very fruitful in what it helped produce happened while I was coaching high school basketball. It was my second week at the school and I had barely learned all of the players' names. I had not learned their personalities yet, but with respect to one player, I was about to. (Sorry for that dangling participle.)

After a week of practice, the head coach divided the players into two teams. We scheduled an intra-squad scrimmage one evening. It was open to the public and since this was a small community, the whole town turned out to watch. Admission consisted of canned goods which were donated to charity.

During that first week, I noticed that one junior – we'll call him Emerson – was a rebounding machine. He was about 6' 2" and weighed a healthy 140. He was a one striper. (…as in, he was so thin he only had one stripe on his pajamas.) He could jump reasonably well and just had a nose for the basketball. He was also high strung. I didn't know the extent of that tendency until the next week.

For this scrimmage, Emerson was on the other team. I looked at the rosters and they were very evenly matched. The best players were the four seniors plus two sophomores and when I looked at the match-ups, I figured they would cancel each other out. Emerson was the wild card. I knew that if he was allowed to go after rebounds unchecked, he would control the boards and that would tilt the balance of the game in his team's favor. We had to stop Emerson.

I had that special assignment but nobody talented enough to execute it. I chose one of my lesser players who was very intelligent. He was well aware that he wasn't very talented, but he did what was asked. The most valuable gift a player has is what's on his shoulders and this kid proved it in this scrimmage. He was the definition of, "coachable."

He was 5' 7" and weighed 120 pounds. (Another one striper.) His assignment was to block out Emerson and not let him get any rebounds. I told him how important this was in determining the outcome of the game. I told him I didn't care if he got a rebound all night. Just be sure Emerson didn't get any. Even though this was just an intra-squad game to generate some excitement in the community, I wanted to win. (I told you I am competitive.)

The game was a struggle for both teams because it was early in the season and the players were playing with strange lineups. The score remained close throughout the game and we won by seven. When I looked at the statistics, I was shocked, amazed, and utterly ecstatic!

116

My small, not-very-talented, single-minded player had held Emerson to one rebound. He got that one meaningless rebound with less than three minutes left in the game and, barring a miracle, the outcome already had been decided. My player had four rebounds of his own. Mission accomplished. The rest of Emerson's game was totally derailed by his frustration at not being, "King of the Rebound," as he liked to think of himself.

At the next practice, the guys were ribbing each other about the outcome of the game. It was all good-natured fun, which is a sign that you've got good camaraderie among the players. I did not see what was lying beneath the surface, soon to boil over.

I had the Junior Varsity (JV) players at one end of the floor. Emerson was with me. The head coach had the other players at the other end of the floor. In one particular drill, it became obvious that Emerson just didn't have his head in the game at all. He was mentally elsewhere...like thinking about Susie from Chemistry class who broke up with him that day.

Somebody said something minor to him like, "Come on Emerson, hold onto the ball." He got mad, turned red in the face like he was about to explode, and said something about not being in the mood to practice that day. I hit the ceiling. I barked at him louder than I had ever talked to any of these kids up to this point. I said, er um, shouted – well, o. k. – I flat out yelled, "EMERSON, THIS ISN'T ABOUT WHAT KIND OF

MOOD YOU'RE IN! THIS IS ABOUT THE TEAM! GET YOUR
MIND ON PRACTICE AND GET IT DONE!

I couldn't believe how quiet it got. The other end of the court
stopped everything. I could tell everybody was looking at me, including
the head coach, but the key in a situation like that is to stay the course. So
I did. I went right on with our drill as if nothing had happened and
Emerson shaped up immediately. The other players were more focused
too. My outburst began to pay dividends but I would not know the full
effect until the next season.

Understand, I'm not a big yeller for disciplinary purposes. If
necessary; sure, but I don't believe in just yelling for the sake of showing
the kids who's boss. I have much better success addressing players very
directly with the expectations of a high level of performance. I don't
expect them to screw around and they don't – very often.

******

Fast-forward a year. Our players were woeful in the ball handling
department. I named a half dozen or so of the worst dribblers and
assigned them a task to be completed before the start of each practice.
Each player was to get two balls and dribble them simultaneously around
the court. They were told to go at their own pace but push as fast as they

could while maintaining control of the balls for two laps. As they got better, their pace would improve. Emerson was one of these players.

In the beginning, there were balls going everywhere. Gradually the players got better. That is the nature of a ball handling drill. Doing it for an hour at a time one day per week is not as valuable as doing it for ten minutes per day.

A couple of the younger players felt that this drill was beneath them. Never mind that they couldn't perform the drill with any proficiency whatsoever. Emerson, on the other hand, attacked the drill with a vengeance. He was a senior so if anyone should have felt like the remedial nature of this drill was a slap in the face; it might have been the older player.

Not Emerson. He showed some real leadership. By doing the drill to the best of his ability each day, he set an example for the younger kids. This is how you do it if you want to get better.

When I commended Emerson on his performance and his attitude regarding that drill, his answer was always the same. "Anything to get better, Coach. Anything to get better." He continued to do this every day before practice without being told.

Early in the season, the prospect of Emerson dribbling the ball during a game caused great consternation for the head coach. (That's a euphemism for saying he would go rudikazooty when Emerson even thought about dribbling.) A couple of times, I was afraid the coach was going to burst that bulging blood vessel in his temple. People in the next county could hear him shout when the ball went to my oldest dribbling tutee. "EMERRRSSSOOONNN!!!!" That was Emerson's cue not to dribble and that he should pass the ball.

Gradually, over the course of the season, I could see Emerson getting much, much better at his ball handling skills. The head coach did not see it since I worked more closely with players on their individual skills. I knew the progress he was making. Emerson routinely told me, "I just want to get better, Coach. Anything to get better." He was also developing confidence in his newly acquired ball handling skills.

The night had come for the last home game in the history of this school. After well over a century of existence, declining enrollment had brought about the inevitable. Our small school was closing. The whole community turned out, including all of the area television stations. This was to be a night to remember.

We were playing a school that had beaten our girls' and boys' teams at their gym earlier in the season. To set the stage, the girls' teams played first. With the crowd providing a raucous atmosphere, our girls not only upset them; we blew them out by 18 points – courtesy of the lady coach whom you read about in the Introduction. (I told you she was good.)

Now it was our turn. With four seniors from the previous season graduated, we relied on two juniors and Emerson. Emerson's job was to rebound and play defense. Oh yes, and to pass the ball (without dribbling) when he got it. How would the high-strung Emerson handle the pressure of this historic night? With all of the hullaballoo, it was anybody's guess how any of our players would respond, much less the slightly jittery Emerson.

The game was a battle from the beginning. Both teams were fighting as if this were the most important game of their lives. Maybe, in a way, it was. The tension continued to mount as the game moved into the second half. The noise in the gym was deafening.

Then, it happened: - that one thing that you dread when your team can't handle the ball very well. The press. By this point, it was obvious to everyone in the gym, including the other team, that we only had two quality ball handlers. That tends to make pressing us rather easy to do. They put on a full court man-to-man press.

We struggled through a few possessions with mixed success. With a tight game, when one team presses, usually one of two things happens. One is that the offensive team gradually finds the weaknesses in the press and has less and less trouble with it as the game continues. The other possibility is that the press rattles the other team and causes turnovers.

Nursing a five point lead with just a couple of minutes left, we took the ball out under their basket. Momentum was squarely on their side after a couple of steals with their press and we were feeling less and less secure with our slim lead. We set up our full court, inbounds play designed to break the press. Our star player would inbound the ball. One player set a screen for our best guard to get open and come to the ball. Meanwhile, Emerson would run toward the ball, then stop, and run a fly pattern – just like in football. Our star saw that Emerson was open and threw a perfect touchdown pass that Emerson caught in stride at the ten-second line.

Now here is where it got really interesting. The entire crowd in that gym held its collective breath. Their fans realized Emerson had nothing between himself and the basket so surely he would try to go the distance. Our fans were likely thinking that he would probably bounce the ball off of his foot and kick it out of bounds.

As our coach panicked and began to scream, "EMERS....," I grabbed a towel to use for compression in case that bulging vein gave way. Emerson never hesitated. He caught the pass over his shoulder like a wide receiver and dribbled full speed to the basket for the uncontested lay-up. He was as confident and graceful as if he were, well, some other confident and graceful player. Nobody had ever seen him do that nor did they expect him to be able to do that…and with the game on the line, no less.

That was the basket that broke our opponent's back. You could see the air get sucked right out of their players. The lead was not insurmountable with the time remaining, but after that play, the momentum had swung our direction and their players now lacked the adrenaline-fueled energy that fed their attack.

It was Emerson's dedication to that menial pain-in-the-neck task of dribbling two basketballs around the gym every day while everyone else was shooting around and having fun that won that game. The fact that he embraced that simple little drill and gave it his best effort every play every day paid big dividends. (He also had twelve rebounds.)

I wasn't done with Emerson. Two weeks later, we were preparing for the state tournament. A random draw set us up for a rematch with that same team. As luck would have it, we would play them for a third time in six weeks.

During our last hard practice before that game, we were working on our offense. The JV players provided the defense. My son was helping us on the JV team. At 6' 3", 225 lbs., he could handle the rebounding chores for us. I say, "us," because due to injuries, I helped also.

We played a modified 2 – 3 zone so I played the middle where I didn't have to move much, which I could no longer do anyway. My game knowledge and surprisingly quick hands compensated for my no longer quick feet. My son guarded our star player everywhere he went so that left the other players to pick up the slack.

On the other side of the ball, Emerson tried to do his part. He tried to drive. I would stop him and, along with a couple of small guards, I would slap at the ball. This was our last full practice and I had some things in mind to prepare Emerson for the game. I was not very particular whether I slapped the ball or Emerson's hands. Either way, he wasn't going to score.

When a shot was missed, I put my broad backside – or as my son called it, my child bearing hips – into Emerson and moved him out to the free throw line. After doing this a number of times, I could sense that someone was staring at me from above.

I'm only 5' 9" and when bent over in a block out position, that made me considerably shorter than Emerson's 6' 2". As I looked up and behind me, Emerson was looking down at me with a bemused look on his face. He was a polite kid so he said nothing, but if there were a thought bubble over his head, it would have said, "What the heck are you doing, Old Man?"

I explained it to him very pointedly (loudly and in a very animated fashion – as is my style). **"Emerson, you aren't going to get any rebounds today. I might not get any either but I don't care about that. The main thing is; you're not getting any. If you're not getting any rebounds, I'm betting my teammates can out rebound your teammates."** I don't think he believed that I could keep him off of the boards but he was beginning to get the message.

The practice continued with more of the same. Emerson tried to drive. There was our defense: hack, hack, and hack some more. Emerson couldn't get any rebounds. Old fat butt here made sure of that. Emerson's stress-o-meter was running higher with each possession. You could see the redness in his face rise like the mercury in a thermometer.

Just as he was about to blow his top, the coach ended practice and called the players over to him. I explained to Emerson exactly what we had done. We put so much pressure on him that he had to work his tail off and no matter what he tried, we had an answer. We had one person solely dedicated to stopping him plus help from two others. If he could survive what we threw at him in that practice, he'd be all right in the game. His pasty white color gradually returned as the bright red 'mercury' drained from his face.

That was our approach to building a competitive attitude in one player. If you look at the many components of the two examples I described with Emerson, you'll see that he learned a lot more than just a specific skill. First, he learned humility, focus, and concentration. Then he was rewarded with some success, only to have that euphoric feeling taken away in that last practice. That was just to prepare him for that tournament game.*

Whatever sport you are coaching, focus and concentration are two of the most important characteristic of the most successful payers. This is never more true than when kids are going through adolescence. It is during those years that kids are convinced that they know far more than they actually do – maybe even more than you, their coach. A player may be physically capable of performing the tasks at hand at a very high level, but he cannot execute physically unless his mind is fully engaged. Forget any multi-tasking mumbo jumbo. An athlete must focus on the matter at hand.

******

Probably the best example of focus and concentration on the part of a player leading to success for the team was not even one of my players. The story was told to me by the player's father.

I had just finished broadcasting a high school basketball game when a gentleman sat down beside me. He asked if there was a way he could get a copy of a previous game broadcast. Our station had broadcast a game for this high school's girls' basketball team the previous Saturday. It was a state tournament game and his daughter was a senior playing in her final season.

I knew that they had won the game by just a few points but I didn't know the details. The man relayed the finish to me. It seems that we were ahead by two points and had the ball. With 30 seconds to go, his daughter was fouled. She averaged 10 points per game but on this day, she had not taken a shot. Not one. No free throws or anything.

She stepped to the line shooting the bonus. The proud father told me he could tell she was focused on the rim and he was confident she would hit the shot. The basket was right in front of the opposing team's cheering section so they were going rudikazooty. The noise was deafening. She hit both shots; the team won the game; and they advanced in the tournament.

The next day at dinner, the girl asked her dad about the game. She said she figured that when she went to the free throw line with the outcome of the game hanging in the balance, the opposing team's fans would be yelling and screaming and basically doing everything they could to make her miss. She then asked her dad, "Why was it so quiet?"

This girl was so focused on her job that she didn't even realize what was going on around her. That's focus. That's concentration. Athletes of all ages can achieve their very best only if they are totally focused. They can't be worried about the crowd or Aunt Betty or Susie from Chemistry class. If you can coach your players to focus to the point where they can block out extraneous noise and distractions, you've given them their best opportunity to be successful.

******

Another very important aspect of shaping players' attitudes can be illustrated by another fullback I once coached. This was the fullback who replaced the one you've already read about. This was the following year and the young man had gone through the same learning curve as my previous fullbacks. He had to learn very quickly how to pick and choose which player to block when leading a sweep. It was trial and error and this guy handled it beautifully.

It was very early in the season so I was still teaching him the finer points of his job. He was a very good blocker and he relished his job and title as, "The Insurance Policy." You see, with seventh graders, on any given pass play, even with the best of offensive lines – and we had the best one around, somebody from the defense will get through the line. I always kept the fullback in the backfield to protect the quarterback. Thusly, he became the quarterback's, *"Insurance Policy."* (Incidentally, we suffered no sacks that season.)

This kid was a very good, powerful runner. He was not particularly fast, but he was a punishing runner. And what does everybody who has ever carried the ball want? The ball. They want more carries. As you could imagine, with several good backs on this team, the team was best served when he was the lead blocker. Still, when we needed the tough, sure yards with low risk, he got the call. He relished this role. Sort of a macho thing I guess.

We were preparing for the mud game. Our opponent had a very fast, strong middle linebacker named Weatherford. (You guessed it: not his real name.) Mr. Weatherford would go on to become a three year starter in high school and a very accomplished 100 meter dash man on his nigh school's track team before going to college on a football scholarship.

In two previous games against this opponent, we lost each by six points. We had the superior line so we opened holes the entire game. The problem was; Weatherford was so quick to the hole that he made the tackle with very little yardage gained.

I devised a special scheme for this playoff game. We would put our fullback in different positions so he could get to the hole first. Wherever we were going to run, he was the first man through the hole.

At the first practice that week, I sat down with the fullback to tell him of our plan. I told him he wasn't going to carry the ball much that Saturday. It wasn't that he hadn't done a good job running the ball; in fact he had done very well. I told him we had a special assignment for him. He looked me right in the eye, grinned, and asked, "Weatherford?"

I couldn't believe it. He couldn't have known what was coming. I had only talked about this plan on the phone with the assistant coach. Still, this kid had gained the understanding that the team needed him to do what he did best. And that was blocking. If that meant not running the ball, he didn't care. He had that special assignment and he relished it. (Again; maybe that macho thing.)

How did he know what this, "special assignment," was? Why did he seize upon this opportunity while cheerfully giving away that thing that running backs covet the most: his carries? Throughout the season, he had heard me talk about the value of each back blocking for the others. He knew his importance blocking on pass plays. My take on touchdown runs is that the big uglies did the dirty work and the backs had the easy part. I never directed anything specific at him with regard to what he should do to make the team better. The message was better received when he added things up for himself. My philosophy is always, "Team first." He inferred what task would be important for us to win this game.

I told him his job on every running play was to go through the hole first, ahead of the ball carrier. I said to skip anybody you see and go find Weatherford. It wouldn't be hard to find him; he'd be coming to you right at the point of attack. Hit him right between the one and the eight, (Weatherford wore 18), and go 'til you hear the whistle.

We taught him where to line up on different plays and by Saturday, he was ready to go. Since this was the mud game, our strong, slow-ish fullback, with his new understanding of how to block his nemesis, had a bit of an edge on the fleet-footed Weatherford. We won the game and our fullback held Weatherford to zero tackles. *ZERO!!!*

The fact that he performed so well was terrific, but that was not the important part. We're talking about shaping athletes' attitudes. This kid was the epitome of the attitude you want in your players. When faced with the prospect that he was not going to get to do the one thing that running backs love the most – carry the ball, he didn't even flinch or hang his head. He understood what the team needed and got excited about the idea. He dove into a very difficult task and did it better than I could ever imagine. If I could bottle and sell that attitude, I'd be rich. His attitude won the game and gave us the championship.

   *Well of course I'm going to tell you about Emerson's tournament game. Did I have you on the edge of your seat? (Be honest.) Our number two player broke his leg in the first quarter and we lost the game by four points. As for Emerson, he had 22 points and 21 rebounds – incredible numbers for a high school game. That performance was far better than we could have asked of him - or any player for that matter. The hard work and that brutal final practice paid off. He will always have the memory of that game, but it would be years before he really understood what he learned about himself during that season.

VIII. Building a Team; Building a Program

Remember in chapter two, I suggested coaching more than one sport in an effort to get to know all available athletes? The more you are involved with the kids, the more you will be able to help them and help your team(s).

I mean really get involved at all age levels. The more you know about all of the players in your program, the better off you will be. If you are a high school varsity coach, take the time to watch the younger players at practice – in all sports. Study their rosters so you know who and what you are watching. Don't waste your time watching some random jerseys running around in circles. Actually *learn* who the players are and learn their skills as they develop them. This will provide benefits to you in future years.

******

One year, I had a very strong football team returning from the previous season. I needed an extra couple of linemen – o. k. I'll take quality linemen any time. They win ball games but more on that later. I also needed a defensive back, specifically a safety, who could defend the pass. In the limited skills exhibition that this league had in place – this is no NFL combine – it was difficult to distinguish who could walk and chew gum, much less intercept a pass.

Since I had also coached basketball for several years and these same athletes also played football, I knew most of the available players. There was a quiet, unassuming boy who was new to football so he didn't know his way around just yet. It was easy for him to get lost in the shuffle. I knew him from coaching him in basketball. None of the other coaches even noticed him.

The thing is, his biggest asset in basketball, besides his terrific attitude, was his ability to play help side defense. He was very adept at cutting off passing lanes and either getting the steal or at least a deflection. That very specific skill translates very well to the safety position in football and it was exactly what I needed. Knowing the players paid dividends in the form of drafting this kid for football. More on him later.

******

One year, the kid I chose to be my quarterback did not want the job. He was (and still is) a shy kid. He didn't want the attention of being the star player – and we made sure he really wasn't. He was merely the best quarterback on the best team in the league – for several seasons. Because I had coached him in other sports, I knew his personality well enough to know how to persuade him to be my quarterback.

Sure, I could have assigned him the position, regardless of what he wanted. Remember, you'll always get better results if the kid actually wants to do what you are asking. You need to get your players on the same page with you so they really want to accept the challenge. In this case, before trying to convince him to play quarterback, I knew he would have to believe that he was the best choice for the position.

First, I talked with him about the physical assets a quarterback must have. The quarterback needed good hands to take snaps without fumbling. He needed some speed because he would be handling the ball a lot and would need to be fast enough to get the job done. He would need to be physically tough enough to take the beating that a quarterback takes in youth football. If he had a good arm, that was a bonus. We wouldn't use it often because in youth football because typically the blocking is not sufficient to allow for much passing. The passing and the catching is not that difficult for kids at that age; the problem is the blocking.

We discussed the players on our team and which one(s) might match our description of a quarterback. All of the players we discussed had some good skills, but none had all of the attributes we needed. He was the only one who had it all. He was big, strong, fast, had a great arm, and hands like toilet seats. His mental acuity was an added bonus that I had no inkling he possessed until I asked him to try the position.

This was a two-way discussion, not like most of the, "discussions," that I had with players. Those were, in actuality, monologues. I talked; they listened. This situation was different. I knew for this kid to be a successful quarterback, he needed to be part of the decision making process. He needed to decide to do it.

After our discussion, he understood why I chose him, why he should do it, and why the team's success depended on him. That's a lot of pressure to put on a young player, but as you'll soon read, I'm the coach who wouldn't let a seven year old rest until we had scored and won the game. *(And that was just a jamboree!)* Basically, he had to buy into the idea of being the quarterback and he had to feel like it was his decision, not mine.

Once my QB understood why he was *the man*, it became his personal goal to be the best he could be. He was determined not to just carry the ball all of the time but to see how many players he could help score touchdowns. That meant distributing the ball to all of the backs evenly. It included the occasional scoring pass to receivers who were not also running backs and therefore had not scored a lot of touchdowns. Because of his overall attitude toward the job of playing quarterback, he was able to put the team first. (Remember that altruism thing?) He was our best runner, but he never led the team in carries. He will tell you to this day that he didn't score any touchdowns; the big uglies did. He just toted the ball for them. The team was more important than the individual. That is the attitude you need to foster in your players.

******

I know you're just itching for another example of what to avoid in your coaching endeavors, so here goes. I once had a kid who was always big and athletic for his age. He was not big like a lineman, but he was big and rawboned and very athletic. He was fast for his size, but more importantly, his feet were extremely quick. In athletics, that combination makes a huge difference in what you're able to accomplish on the field(s) or court.

In fact, in high school, he participated in varsity football, basketball, and track. He was 6' 3" and 225 lbs. with those very quick feet. Of all of the things he did athletically, the most extraordinary thing he did was throw the discus *and* run the 110 meter high hurdles in the *same* track meets. (Let that sink in for a moment.) He also ran a leg of the 4x100 meter relay. I think he set the record for the heaviest high hurdler in our city's history.

The point here is that this athlete was extremely versatile. As a coach, I'd have been licking my chops to work with an athlete like that. With that strength and quickness combination, he was a very difficult matchup in basketball, but his coach made an error in judgment fairly common among coaches. One look at the boy's build told the coach that he was a power forward. Put him on the block and expect him to stand there.

Never mind that he was the fastest player on the team in an eighty-four foot race. (That's the length of a high school basketball court.) One of his teammates was also on the track team. This player could run the 400 meters in 49 seconds so, yes, he was *faaaassst!!!*

Still, in a length of the court sprint, the 225 pounder was the fastest player on the team,...but let's put him on the block and have him stand there. One of our main goals as coaches is to maximize the potential of each player and by extension, the potential of the team. This coach got caught up in the physical appearance of the athlete and not the actual talent of the player and his potential contribution to the team.

As for the 400 meter man, he had extremely quick hands to go along with those amazing feet. He was the best open court defender on the team but he went underutilized as well. He fell victim to another problem that runs rampant in the coaching world. He played the same position as one of the coaches' sons. (Sorry for his bad luck.)

So here you have two extremely good athletes with excellent basketball skills. They sat the bench. Why? Because the coach *chose his players; he did not let the competition choose them.* He never assessed the skills of his players. Heck, He didn't even **know** the skills of his players.

In one game, the city's leading scorer lit his team up for 38 points – 17 over his average - while being guarded by the aforementioned assistant coach's son. I had occasion to talk to the coach some time after that game. We discussed the game and the tough rivalry loss.

I praised the scoring ability of the city's leading scorer. Although he was an excellent scorer, he was not physically imposing, nor was he particularly quick. He should not have been that tough of a matchup for this team. While tiptoeing around the issue of how overmatched the coach's son was in trying to guard him, I asked this coach who was the best athlete on the team. He didn't know. He had no idea. HOW COULD A COACH BE THAT CLUELESS!?! You have to know that this is another example of *what to avoid!*

I gave those two player examples to illustrate one very important point. That is, when you are putting together a team, look at the specific skill set that each player has. Don't get locked into first impressions based on looks. Not only is this a good rule for dating; it works for evaluating athletes too.

******

When you are looking at putting together a team, the first thing to do is assess the overall talent. Take basketball for example. If you have a team full of giraffes coming back, don't plan to run a guard oriented offense. Or, if you have a group of players who are very fast and are great ball handlers, you'll want to shape the team and its strategy to capitalize on those skills.

I know this sounds overly simplistic but you'd be surprised how often the best talent goes unrecognized by coaches. They skip the rudimentary step of itemizing the players' specific skills.

One way to do this is to write specific basketball (or whatever sport) skills on a board and list the players in order from best to worst for each category. Have all of the coaches provide input and come to a consensus of opinion. You will probably have the same player(s) at the tope of several categories. That's to be expected and it is not necessarily a bad thing. It helps you identify interchangeable players based on their skills.

Maybe you have two players at one position who are very close in their abilities to play that position. At another position, there is not much depth but the best player at this position is also the best player at the first position. What makes your team the best? Maybe you play your second best player at the first position and put the best one at that position in the other position. That way, you cover two positions very well instead of having the absolute best at one position and a definite weak spot in the other position.

Writing players' skill sets on a chalkboard is a great exercise to give you a visual layout of the talent you will have at your disposal. From there, you can begin to move the pieces of the puzzle into positions. This sounds positively elementary my dear Watson, but too many coaches don't do it.

Their egos make their choices, not the abilities of the players. I once watched a high school JV team with a very tall starting front line of 6' 6", 6' 5", and 6' 4" play against a team whose tallest player was 6' 1". The coach ran his typical, "Four Out," offense against the much shorter team. Four Out is just what it sounds like and it takes too many of your big galoots away from the basket, thus hurting your rebounding. Surprise! They lost that game. You know where I'm going with this: another example of *what to avoid!*

******

Let's look at yet another example of what to avoid. Think about what you would do if you had a freshman point guard with excellent court vision and tremendous passing ability. And what would you do if he grew to be 6' 4" by the time he was a junior?

140

Good court vision is a very rare commodity and if you've got a good passing guard who has it, by all means, give him the ball and let him run your offense. Let's also consider that you have three other players who are 6' 5" or taller. All are capable of starting. Your 6' 4" passer is probably your best player, especially now with his added height.

Let me point out that in this region of the country, high school guards are generally less than 6' tall and if they reach 6' or better, they are considered tall for the position. Your excellent passing guard is no longer short. He's 6' 4" for crying out loud! In addition to his terrific court vision, now he can see over his defenders. Well, you guessed it. Instead of utilizing this kid's excellent - and now improved - passing ability (you know, due to that height thing), the coach moved the player inside. That meant benching one of his taller post players and inserting a short guard to replace the tall guard that he moved under the basket.

Let's look at what you've got now. You've got your best player in an unfamiliar position; you've taken away his strongest asset; and you've reduced the size of your team on the floor. All of that was because the coach saw that his best player was now tall and he forgot about the skill set that player had developed. Another good example of *what to avoid!*

If you've been following along, you may have had a light bulb moment with that last example. Here we had a guard. He had always been a guard. He learned the game of basketball from the perspective of a guard. Then, something amazing happened. Puberty kicked in.

141

Yes, adolescence can be a beautiful thing in the development of an athlete. It can also bumfuzzle coaches. As we've seen, some coaches pigeonhole players at an early age. Then, when a player hits his growth spurt, it's too late because the coach made his decision about the player several years earlier.

This coach did not make that mistake because he wasn't afraid to change the player's position. He made a different mistake. He got all excited with the fancy new exterior and forgot to look under the hood. Had this player stayed similar in size relative to the other players, the coach would have left him at point guard running the team. He would have been very good for the team under those circumstances. With the added height, he would have been even better at the point guard spot. As it was, he was very ordinary as a post player and the coach did not have another good point guard on the team. (I'm shaking my head in disbelief now.)

******

Many players do not develop an exceptional talent at an early age. It takes some time, and maybe it takes that growth spurt and some maturity for a player's talent to really blossom. How many players don't stick it out long enough for all of the pieces to fall into place? With all of the other options kids have these days, they can find other uses for their time rather than running their tails off every day at some practice just so they have a front row seat at the games. (That would be on the bench.)

There is a very simple way to avoid losing a player at an early age. Keep more players. See? I told you it was simple. Take football for example. If you can keep fifty 8th grade football players, maybe you can hope to have 25 by the time they're seniors. All situations are different but that is an optimistic estimate.

I have coached with a middle school basketball coach who once kept 21 players *on a basketball team*. He did this because many of them were very close in ability and he didn't want to *guess* which players would grow, develop further, and stick with basketball vs. which ones would move on to pursue other interests. With this group, after the first three or four players, there was not a significant drop-off in talent through twenty kids. Obviously you look at your talent break and adjust accordingly. (I have also been involved with the same age groups where I was all for keeping only 12 – 14 kids due to the lack of talent.)

This coach always said it was better to act in favor of the players, not the convenience of the coaches. I can tell you it was tough on the coaches to keep ten players on an "A" team and eleven on a "B" team, but that didn't matter to him. The kids deserved the opportunity to compete and he wasn't going to pigeonhole them at a young age. That's the kind of coach to emulate and here's one specific example of why.

I took the "B" team this particular year. The objective with a "B" team is multifaceted. You want to give as many players as much playing time as possible through a series of "B" games with other schools. You also have the opportunity to take a struggling "A" player with the "B" team to work on specific issues of weakness with the goal of getting him back to the "A" squad as soon as possible. Also, if the "A" game is particularly close, there may be some of those players who did not play much, if at all. Those players would then come to me for the "B" game. Sometimes I had 12 or more players to play.

With that many players, I told them we were going to "Loyola Marymount" our opponents the entire game. That's when their eyes glazed over. Come on guys. Paul Westhead? Hank Gathers? Bo Kimble? Is anybody home? Not a light bulb went on among 'em. O. K., so it was in 1989 – 90, well before any of these kids were born, when LMU set an NCAA scoring record averaging 122.4 points per game while scoring over 100 points in 28 0f 32 games. Loyola Marymount was not all gimmick though, as they advanced in the NCAA Tournament to the final eight before losing to eventual champion UNLV. In other words, we were going to run teams out of the gym.

The point of the history lesson was to give them a tangible example (well, it was tangible to me) of what you could do with lots of players and lots of substitutions. With so many players, I expected every one of them to go as hard as possible every second, knowing they would be coming out in a couple of minutes. If they didn't hustle – and I mean *HUSTLE* – they made their decision to enjoy a front row seat with me. (Their decision, not mine.)

It wasn't long before the kids got the hang of the system. The kids actually thanked me for substituting. For my way of thinking, every player should want to play every second of every game, but still they must understand that they need to rest periodically. That's normally the battle you fight, but not with my system.

It seems in previous seasons, they would be playing for such a long stretch of time they were exhausted. They began pacing themselves. *Every* player who ever plays any sport learns how to rest in some area of the game. My message was that you can rest on the bench, but if you're in the game, you had better be giving every last bit of effort you can muster.

I was not unrealistic in my expectations. It was sort of a trade off; if they gave every ounce of effort, they would come out before actually throwing up and they would go back in as soon as possible. They still got a lot of playing time but it was broken up into shorter stints where they could play at a higher level without fatigue setting in too badly.

This speed approach pushed some players out of their comfort zone. That's what I wanted. I didn't want players playing at the Sunday afternoon church league pace. I wanted them to learn to function mentally and physically at a much faster pace than on their previous teams.

Before you raise your hand to point out what I have missed, please bear with me. There is an exception to every rule. (I am not totally stupid.) We had two big uglies – space eaters – aircraft carriers, whatever you call them. They were not built for speed. I used them as one player. I kept a close eye on them and platooned them more frequently than the rest of the players. You can't expect your Clydesdales to keep up with your cheetahs.

This approach provided another benefit. One of the smartest kids on the team was a guard with all of the speed of a tortoise (of Tortoise and Hare fame). The problem was that while he was figuring things out, the other team had continued playing and my guy came up short time after time.

I had a tough time believing that he was that slow because he was a very good soccer player. Now I might make disparaging remarks about soccer players, (Everyone learns to use their feet to walk, usually around their first birthday; then most people move on and learn to use their hands), but I'll take a soccer player on my teams every chance I get. You can count among their assets exceptional conditioning, good footwork, and excellent speed.

I discussed these issues with the guard in question and I thought he understood. Still, his play did not keep pace with what I wanted. I was about to conclude that maybe I was expecting more than he had to give. Then it happened.

In a tight game, a loose ball was kicked and went rolling ahead of everybody toward our opponents' goal. The nearest player was one of their players who could have had an easy steal and lay-up. Well, Slowpoke took off like a shot, ran past the opposing player, and retrieved the ball. It was an amazing display of speed and power as his strides ate up the floor and he reeled in the other player to get the errant ball.

After that game, we discussed his speed issue again. O. K., this wasn't a discussion so much as it was a monologue – and I was the speaker. He finally got it and we had a good laugh at the expense of the poor kid on the other team who my guy just smoked in a fifty-foot race. Take that, other kid! (See, I told you I am competitive.)

Anyway, he was a part-time starter for me and remained so throughout the season – and this was on an 8th grade "B" team. Over the summer, he hit a growth spurt and developed even more speed playing soccer. The following year, as a freshman in high school, he started on the JV team. Isn't puberty a wonderful thing? If we would have kept only 12 – 15 players on the eighth grade team, I doubt that he would have been one of them. That's a great testament to keeping more players than what is convenient for the coaches.

******

That was one example about one kid. How many of those do you think there are at other schools? How many of those kids are walking the halls instead of playing sports for their schools? I have seen times when I could walk the halls of various high schools, pick a basketball team, and go beat the head coach and his varsity roster. Sadly, I must admit it's not because of my stellar coaching ability; it's because there are too many talented kids who have been pushed aside because of some shortsighted coaches.

In order to build a strong high school program, you need to look at what it takes to keep your pipeline of players full. Remember, you don't want to have a great team every few years and not much in between. In order to keep your pipeline full, you need for young players to grow up wanting to play for your varsity team.

To do that, you need a broad base of players at younger age levels because we know that many of them will opt for other distractions as they grow up. (There's that darn Susie from Chemistry class again distracting your athletes.) The other thing that you have to give players is the opportunity to compete.

I don't mean that after you've picked which players are going to play which positions, you let them practice together. I mean you take the time to learn the players' skill set first and then evaluate them. In that way, you let the players decide, through competition, which ones will be playing come game night.

Have you ever known of a team where there is some level of dissention because the best players are not playing? Players always know who deserves to play and when coaches play the players they've chosen instead of putting the best team on the field (or floor), it erodes the credibility of the coach. Don't kid yourself; the players always know who's the best. They may not understand the game from your perspective yet, but they definitely know who the best players are.

Kids can see through a coach's veneer. They'll know before they even get to the high school level if what a coach says has any validity. The best way for your program to have the momentum to perpetuate its high level of performance is to continually have plenty of good players willing to compete for you. Your best technique for ensuring that attitude is to give them the only thing a true athlete would ever ask of you. That is the *opportunity to compete* for his position.

IX. That Championship Season

We've eliminated the negative aspects of coaching. (*What to avoid.*) We've learned how to establish our expectations of parents and their contributions to the season's success. We've gotten all of our players on board with the foundation of the program and how they will conduct themselves. The players understand what they need to do in order to have the best opportunity to succeed in your system.

You've made a habit of evaluating players' skills, regardless of who they are or how hot their moms are. You've taught them how to think the game, not just do exactly what you tell them to do. (Go stand on the block.) You've established standards for which all team members will strive. The players all know that they are competing against their own potential and for the potential of this team.

You have players wanting to play for you because of your fair but no nonsense attitude. Your program is strong and the pipeline of players eager to perform in your system is full. It seems to me like it's time to see what happens when you put it all out on the field. Contrary to the title of

150

this chapter, we'll actually look at bits and pieces from several different championship seasons.

Before I get into what I told you this chapter is about, I should explain another aspect that mostly stays behind the scenes. One thing I have not mentioned much is the psychological gamesmanship that goes on among coaches within a given league. Some coaches are loaded with bravado. (i. e., massive egos.) They're anxious to tell everyone who will listen just how great their team is, arguably so the rest of the league will be impressed with how good they are as coaches. Other coaches are more apt to downplay the quality of their own team a la Lou Holtz. (You knew when Lou Holtz teams were really loaded because that is when he spent the most time telling you how weak they were.)

I have always figured on two things. First, I do not know everything so the more I listened to other coaches and their techniques, the more information I would have. From there, I would pick and choose what I thought would work – and a lot of that was based on how smart the other coach was. (i. e., whether he was an idiot or not.) I mean, if a very smart person gives you advice in his field of expertise, you should probably listen. On the other hand, if the village idiot tries to wax eloquence on the paradox of Schrodinger's cat, you might not pay much heed.

The second thing is that if the other coaches didn't perceive my team as a threat, they would shift their focus to the other teams in the league, which they perceived to be stronger. I also did not want to give away any trade secrets. (i. e., we've got a killer reverse!) Throughout all of this, I was always, *always* very respectful of other teams, their players, and their efforts. O. k., I guess I cited more than two things, but you get the idea.

During a given week of practice, when I could sense that a group of coaches was about to discuss the merits of the various teams in the league, I immediately joined the conversation. My tactic was to make a preemptive statement about how poorly my team was doing in some specific area.

I would complain about how my players had lost focus or weren't working hard for the team or anything else I could think of to throw them off the trail. Since I routinely asked for help with various drills and techniques, I would ask coaches how they dealt with this problem or that problem. (Usually a made up problem.) It was always a comfortable segue from their intended topic and they were always glad to help a coach in need. I did not derail their conversation, other than to interject the message that my team was not particularly strong. After that, I was all ears, hoping to gather any additional information on their teams.

My players were well aware of my tactics. I told them how I approached the other coaches with regard to my team's progress. They were told to keep that to themselves lest my secret be revealed. I didn't want one of my fake criticisms to get back to a specific player, "through the grapevine." Kids can be fragile and I didn't want any damage to have been done by the time I'd have had the chance to talk with the player to let him know I was just baiting the hook for the other coaches. At practice, my players often traded humorous stories they had heard from other players in the league. These stories consisted of wildly exaggerated negative statements I supposedly said about my own team. My players knew the truth so they enjoyed this little joke on the rest of the league.

This was my modus operandi on all of my teams in any sport. I got better at it the longer I coached. You can't go too far in your criticism or it will become obvious and your sandbagging efforts will become transparent. You just want to sound genuine in your concern for how average (or worse) your team is, hopefully garnering sympathy along the way.

Another part of the psychological aspect of coaching comes in how you deal with your own team. You spend a lot of time with them, much more so than the occasional bull sessions with the other coaches. You have to keep them positive but they must know that they have not reached that goal of playing to their potential. The better my teams got; the harder that became.

I once had the best running back in the football league but I couldn't let him know that. I dropped in enough comments throughout the season about how fast another back was and if he ever got loose against us, we had nobody who could catch him. That was probably true, but the faster back was not nearly as tough as ours was. He also wasn't as coachable. I would not have traded my back for two of the other guy. Keeping my back humble and hungry was somewhat difficult but we made it work. We finished 10 – 0 and won the championship. He went on to start three years for his high school and was All-City twice, before going on to play in college. I knew how good he could be before he did.

******

Let's go all the way back to a youth team. We didn't know it at the time, but our team of 7, 8, and 9 year olds would produce 10 high school starters, some for multiple seasons, and five who would play in college. While other teams at this age level usually had two or three quality players, we had those ten plus another half dozen who could play. Looking back, if we would have been less than undefeated champions, the coaches should have hung our heads in shame.

We started the season with a jamboree game. We played the second best team in the league. Each game consisted of one half of playing time. Each team would start its possession on the fifty yard line. Each possession would last as long as the drive continued. Coaches were allowed on the field behind the offense to help with play calling and alignment.

I had a big advantage here. Our quarterback had a sixth sense about the game. You know how sometimes you see a kid who, from an early age, is a whiz at math, music, or reading? Well, this kid could read a football field like nobody's business. When he got to high school, his instincts were far ahead of his high school coaches so all they knew how to do was tell him to, "go stand on the block," so to speak.

I had worked with our quarterback on when to call which plays. I did not want to send plays in with alternating tight ends, wrist coaches, smoke signals, or carrier pigeons. The QB knew we started with a fullback off tackle to the right, then something to the other side, then back to the right with a sweep. Basically, give the defense a lot of variety to look at, while emphasizing our right (strongest) side.

He bounced things around to the different backs but kept running the sweep right more frequently than other plays. This was to establish that play as our money play. Other teams would have to key on that play or we would pound them into submission with it. (Always nice to talk about athletes this age getting pounded into submission, right?)

If a team didn't load up that side of the field to stop our sweeps, we would continue to run it and score easily. Once they shifted, we ran our killer reverse. You may have read about it previously. My goal was to get our QB to call all of his own plays. He understood the game well enough to intuitively figure these things out. Like the reading prodigy or the math whiz, this kid was way ahead of the other kids in the league in

155

his understanding of the game. Yes, this kid could read a football field. (And yes, he did go to college on a football scholarship.)

When the jamboree was upon us, I asked the QB if he wanted me on the field. He looked me right in the eye and said very calmly and confidently, "No. I've got it." He did too. We moved the ball all over the place and basically beat the snot out of our opponent. By contrast, the other team only got one first down the entire time. Still, with just under a minute to play, the game remained scoreless. We had run up and down the field on them, but we had penalties at the worst possible times so we never got the ball into the end zone.

Wit 55 seconds left, we started a new possession at the fifty yard line. Our first play was the fullback off right tackle for fifteen yards. That play is normally good for 5 – 7 yards and establishes a short yardage situation on second down. This time it went for a fifteen yard gain and changed things dramatically. It gave us a first down on the thirty-five with 48 seconds left.

I called time out. In the huddle, one of my rookie seven year old linemen looked at me huffing and puffing and said, "Coach, I'm tired. I need a rest." I looked at him, pointed at the clock and said, "Bruce, we've got 48 seconds left. We're going to the end zone. You can be tired after we score." He shook his head and said, "O. k., coach." (Of course Bruce is not his real name, and yes he also went to college on a football scholarship.)

We ran a couple more plays and got to the seven yard line with 11 seconds left. I used our last time out. Our opponent had two studs. They put one at each defensive end position to keep us from running our sweeps. Their right end was the weaker of the two so I elected to run our sweep left, directly at him.

He was very tough to block so I substituted a backup lineman (remember green trash can boy?) at right guard, and moved that guard to the left wing back spot. I told him to line up in the backfield on our left end's hip. His assignment was to put his facemask right between the 2 and the 1 on that kid's jersey (He wore # 21) and drive him to the sideline. Don't stop until the whistle and don't look to see what else is happening.

The QB pitched to the future All-City running back, and then led the blocking around the left end. With our QB and fullback hitting anything in the other colored jersey, the ball carrier waltzed, untouched, into the end zone. We won 6 – 0.

My assistant coach asked what happened to #21 and I had to admit I had no idea. I never saw him. When we watched the film, we saw that our former guard, now our *permanent* fullback locked onto #21 and drove him clean out of the camera view. If you've ever seen a youth league game, you'll know that most blockers stand up and turn around to see what's going on behind them. That's a big no-no – at any level of football. This kid did not do that. He did what he was told – and he did it better than I could have imagined.

Some people might think that a jamboree game is insignificant and maybe I should have let the tired lineman sit out a few plays. Remember how we go about setting our expectations? We were clearly better than the other team. They were the second best team in the league, but on this day, we kicked the ever-loving snot out of them. We deserved to win. I wanted to make sure we did.

Our tired guard learned how to dig a little deeper, fight through the fatigue, and finish the job. Our new fullback understood the importance of blocking the other team's stud. He readily accepted the responsibility of such an important role. He would come through for us like that many times during the season. The players learned how to stay calm, do their jobs, and band together as a team. Those are some very valuable lessons that served these kids well throughout many years of football and many other aspects of their lives. Mentally, we had forged a very strong platform on which to build the rest of the season.

******

We would go on to finish the season undefeated and face this same team in the championship game. Before that game, I called my coaches together and told them that our jobs were done. That confused the heck out of them. I continued to explain myself. I told them that the players had worked hard all season and had learned their positions. If they didn't know what to do now, it's too late. This game was in their hands. The coaches agreed.

We did not look sharp in the first half. We just didn't run like a well-oiled machine. All teams in all sports regardless of age have days like that. (Heck, so do all people everywhere and as I get older, I have more and more of them.) With a couple of minutes remaining in the first half, we were tied at 6 – 6. We had the ball on our own 35 yard line at the left hash mark and were driving.

Our QB is calling all of the plays, as was the norm for our team. We were moving the ball very well, but all of the plays were to our right side, which was toward our sideline. I couldn't figure out why he was not mixing things up and calling something to the left side. After a few more plays, we had the ball on their 35 yard line and the ball was on the right hash mark.

As our QB was calling the next play, you could hear the coaches yelling from the other sideline, "REVERSE! WATCH THE REVERSE!" Our team went to the line of scrimmage. The QB walked up to the center, looked at all of the players to make sure they were properly set before calling the cadence. He then did something that he had never done before. He turned away from the center, walked back to the running back behind him, and whispered something.

The QB went back to the center and called the cadence. He took the snap, pitched the ball to the running back moving to the right. The guard pulled and the QB went out in front of the running back. It was a sweep right. But there was something very odd about the way the running back was carrying the ball. He had his right arm stretched out with the ball in it, showing everybody in the place that he was going to hand off for the reverse. That was terrible technique. You just don't do that. You hide the ball and make a quick hand off, then continue running as you carry out your fake. *What the heck was he doing?!?*

At this point, I looked at my assistant coach, (who was also the running back's father), and I asked him, *"What the heck is he doing?!?"* His answer: "I don't know." Our wingback, Weatherford – yes the same one who became an opponent in the older youth league – approached to take the handoff. Not so fast, spectators. Just as the exchange was about to take place, our running back tucked the ball safely under his arm and kept it. Weatherford wasn't expecting that to happen, but he did what he was taught. He carried out his fake. *Always carry out your fakes.* He continued running the reverse as if he had the ball.

By then, the opposing coaches were screaming, "REVERSE, REVERSE, *REVEERRRSSSE*!!!" As Weatherford proceeded to run the reverse without the ball, he was greeted – and tackled - by both of our opponent's studs. Meanwhile, our running back scooted untouched into the end zone. With that touchdown, we took a 13 – 6 lead at half time.

That play got our team out of its funk and broke open the game. We went on to win 33 – 6.

It was after the game when we finally cornered our backs to find out what the QB said to the running back before that play. The QB said he had called all of the plays to the right to get the ball to the right hash mark to set up the reverse. He had called the reverse and when he got to the line of scrimmage, he saw that the other team had put both studs on their right, (our left), side. They were primed for our reverse.

He knew Weatherford would get clobbered, which he did, and the play wouldn't work. Instead of letting the play go as called, he turned to the running back, told him to fake the reverse, keep the ball, and keep on running. The running back took it upon himself to hold the ball out and announce to the world that we were running the reverse. Weatherford knew to carry out his fake, although he wasn't too happy about getting tackled by both studs when he was just the decoy. Every aspect of the play worked perfectly.

The dominoes started falling with the QB calling the audible at the line of scrimmage. The running back added his flair to the ruse and Weatherford did something many high school, college, and even pro players don't always do. He carried out his fake at full speed to keep the deception going. All three of those guys would go on to play college football. (Brilliant coaching on my part, right?) O. k., so talented players always make a coach look good.

161

One other footnote to that season came when I coached the all-star team. At our first all-star practice, a coach asked what system we would use to get the plays into the game. At first I was confused because I didn't know what the problem was since my QB called the plays. He suggested using tight ends to message the plays in. I told him the plays were already in the game. The QB calls them. It came as a shock to all of the other coaches in the league to learn that he called our plays. The other coaches had tried all season to see what method we were using to signal, or otherwise get our plays into the game.

They were not aware of the budding young prodigy we had on our team. As I have mentioned, we were loaded with talent. We also taught our players how to think the game and it was never more evident than when we called, then perfectly executed, a fake reverse that we had never even practiced. Never practiced? Heck, the coaches had never even thought of it. That's what can happen when your players know *why* they're doing something instead of just standing on the block.

******

A few years later, I had another really talented team. This time, it was in the upper league. We had the best hogs in the league, my prodigy QB, and several other players from that earlier championship team. This team was strong throughout the roster, but there was one other team that

162

was capable of beating us. They proved it twice during the regular season by one touchdown each time.

As we approached the playoffs, I had the good fortune to talk with Pro-Bowler and Super Bowl winning quarterback, Joe Theismann. He was a speaker at a Chamber of Commerce banquet in our city. Since I worked for the Chamber, I was able to meet Mr. Theismann after the banquet.

I told him that I coached a youth football team and that we were heading into the playoffs. I asked if he would mind if I used a motivational story he had told as a pep talk for my team. He was very gracious and flattered to have me use his story. I then told him that of course if we won the game, then that speech was my own creation. If we lost the game, well that was just some story Joe Theismann told me. I'm not sure if he appreciated the humor, but he acted as if he did. We won, so naturally I took all of the credit.

Let's go to our championship game that season. We had avenged our two losses during the mud game by holding Weatherford to zero tackles. Now, for the championship game, we were looking at beautiful weather and a fast playing surface. We were playing a good team, but a team we should defeat rather easily nonetheless. However; they had the fastest player on the field and as always, with time on the clock, the fastest player can always find the end zone.

In the first quarter, we had a beautifully executed 75 touchdown pass called back because of a meaningless clip. It was a good call. Our receiver was streaking to the end zone with the ball and no defender near him, when one of our players who was fifteen yards behind, reached out and pushed an opponent in the back. *Aaaarrrggghhhh!!!!*

We had several other easy scoring passes dropped. We had good receivers and that prodigy quarterback. We had not relied heavily on the pass during the season. We had passed enough to know that we could do it effectively. We also avoided one of the most difficult aspects of the passing game: the dastardly ineligible receiver downfield penalty. We didn't have one all season – a testament to how good our hogs were. We came out throwing in the first half of this championship game.

Looking at the championship, no coach would have thought to prepare to defend the pass against us, nor could they have done it effectively anyway. I figured we could pass in the first half and open up a good lead, then run the ball in the second half, continue to score, and eat the clock.

Well, anybody who has been around sports knows that the longer a good team allows a lesser team to stay close, the harder it becomes for the better team to pull away. The lesser team believes it can win and the better team just can't get its rhythm established. That was happening to us before our very eyes. With our senseless penalty and countless drops –

both uncharacteristic of our team - we were mired in a scoreless tie at the half.

In the third quarter, we had them pinned near their own end zone. They were forced to punt. Our QB and one of the mighty mite tacklers were back to return the punt. The QB caught it and my assistant and I were screaming at him to run our way. The field looked wide open to the left side – our side. Naturally, mighty mite and the QB headed to the right side. (Kids just never listen.)

Fifty-five yards later, as mighty mite blocked one defender into another one at the goal line, the QB trotted into the end zone for the TD. The PAT failed, but we led 6 – 0. I asked the QB why they went right when it was open to the left. He replied, "Kurt said, 'follow me,' so I did."

Nobody can say I don't practice what I preach. Those players could see the field a lot better than I could so my opinion as to which side they should run, was irrelevant. Kurt was playing with me for his sixth season and the QB was in his seventh season with me. How about that faith in one's teammate to follow him just because he was told to do so? I was very impressed with both players for their teamwork. You try to develop that faith in one another among your players but you don't always know if it sinks in. This was a great example of two players who paid attention along the way.

Fast forward to the early part of the fourth quarter. We were still clinging to that six point lead. This time, they had us pinned on our own thirteen yard line facing third down. We had developed a very good reverse pass. We didn't have a suitable speedster to run a regular reverse like the other team with which you are now familiar, so we had to take advantage of our QB's talents and run a reverse pass.

This play started like a sweep left. (Our QB was left-handed.) The linemen knew that they must hold the line of scrimmage on a pass play or they would draw a penalty. On the regular sweep, they were free to go downfield and head hunt anyone in the running lane.

The tight end on the right side was green trash can boy. (Not his real name.) At the snap of the ball, he was to give a brush block to the defensive end then let him through. Our tight end was to run up field just to an opening, then turn to find the quarterback. If there were a defensive back covering him, he would have run a skinny post or a square in to the spot on the field that was vacated by the middle linebacker

By the time we ran this play in any game, we had run our sweep left a couple of times so our opponent never expected a reverse pass. Nobody ever stayed home with the tight end. By simply turning toward the quarterback and looking for the ball, the tight end increased the likelihood that the pass would be completed. Plus, he knew how to get open if he were covered.

We had a defensive back who was a very good receiver and had far more speed than our tight end. The plan was to substitute him for the tight end when we ran the reverse pass. I was thinking this would be the perfect time for this play, but the QB had called a play and was breaking the huddle before I could get the substitute into the game.

I had no idea what play he called until I watched it unfold. It was the reverse pass. The perfect play call. Perfectly executed to the starting tight end, *aka* green trash can boy. He was wide open, caught the pass, and was running for the end zone like his life depended on it. Remember, our opponent had the fastest player in the league. Needless to say, this foot race was a mismatch, but green trash can boy had a big head start.

Later, I asked the QB why he didn't substitute for the faster player on that play. He told me he didn't want to tip off the other team that anything special was coming. He also said he knew green trash can boy would catch the pass and we would have a big gain on the play. Once again, the QB had thought things through very well and showed tremendous confidence in his teammate.

And now, back to the play. Give the opposing speedster credit; even facing a long race that he might not win, he never gave up the chase. He made the tackle on the seven yard line. The play had gone for eighty yards. We had been backed up near our own goal line, sure to give them good field position if we couldn't get a couple of first downs. Now, we were knocking on the door of their end zone, ready to punch it in for a touchdown and a two score lead. That reverse pass was the perfect call and the perfect execution at the perfect time.

They held us on four downs at the three yard line. (I did not see that coming.) We helped them out with a penalty in there, but no matter. We were clinging to a six point lead midway through the fourth quarter and they had the fastest player on the field. Any play could have gone for a touchdown because if he got loose, we couldn't have caught him.

Two short gains netted them five yards. On third and five, they ran a sweep right with Mr. Speedster carrying the ball. Our left side defensive back, Mighty Mite B who always turned in opponents' sweeps, got blocked – something that rarely occurred. What a time for that to happen! We had no outside containment. Green trash can boy was in at left defensive end and he was not fast enough to make the play. Somehow, he did it anyway. He shot up field and got Mr. Speedster before he could turn the corner. Loss of two on a great defensive play!

Facing fourth and seven on their own six yard line, they lined up to punt. Great! We held. What a relief! They snapped the ball as whistles blew stopping the play. We had jumped offside.

Now with a fourth and 2, they elected to go for it. Time was running short and they figured they had a good chance of keeping possession. If they punted, they would definitely give us good field position, and with it, the game. I took the opportunity to insert my starting defensive end and pull green trash can boy. Also, this gave me an opportunity to congratulate him on what a great play he had just made. (Remember, I believe very strongly in positive reinforcement.) They called time out so I ran onto the field.

When I got to my team, every one of them was telling me that green trash can boy did not jump offside. They all assumed that I had pulled him to yell at him because of the mistake. Here was a kid who sometimes got under other players' skin, but when they thought he was going to get blamed for something he didn't do, the team rallied around him. They had learned what it meant to be good teammates. When you have a bond like that, it has a synergistic effect on the whole team. I was very proud of them for that, but we still had work to do.

We huddled up. Before I could say anything, our center spoke. He was the biggest kid in the league. He was the best center/nose guard in the league by far. He was also a straight "A" student and very soft-spoken. I could barely hear him but what he said was this. "When we get the ball back, their middle linebacker has been showing blitz in the guard/tackle gaps. I can block my man to whichever side he chooses and we can run it up the middle." I told our QB to call a quarterback sneak on our first play.

There were three very important points here. First, this otherwise shy kid spoke up in the first place when most kids would have been afraid to address a coach in this situation. Second, he had recognized that the tendency of a key player on the opposing team would give us the opening we needed. Third, he used the word, "When." He did not say, "*If* we get the ball back…," he said, "*When…*" He knew we would stop them. That kind of a player is what you hope to have by the end of a season. You don't want your players to be so intimidated by the player/coach dynamic that they are afraid to speak up when they have something important to add.

We held them to no gain on fourth down. On our first down from the eleven yard line, we ran a quarterback sneak. Their middle linebacker blitzed our left side guard/tackle gap and opened up the middle of the field. Our center blocked their nose guard to the left, opening up a huge gap for our QB. He got caught at the one, but we had a first and goal.

Our Mighty Mite A, the one in his seventh year with me, ran it in for the touchdown. He also caught a pass for the extra point. We led 13 – 0 with not much time left. The game was ours. It was fitting that, in this championship game, the two players who were playing their seventh season together scored all of our points.

I went into a little more detail with some aspects of this chapter, but I felt it was necessary to illustrate the mental contributions of some of the players. The attitudes that had developed among the players were critical to the teams' successes. The players were smart, selfless, worked well together, and most importantly they believed in each other. To this day, if you were to ask our QB how many touchdowns he scored in (pick a season or game), he would tell you none. He might have toted the ball, but the big uglies up front scored the touchdowns.

X. Does That Stuff Really Work?

And

Now That it's Over, What Have We Got to Show for it?

I have always been a logical thinker. I approach most situations in life like that. I try to look at the task at hand, determine what the goals are, and form a plan to accomplish those goals in the most expeditious way possible.

Look at cooking a fried chicken dinner. You don't start with the gravy. First you turn on the gas burner to get the iron skillet hot while you are preparing the chicken. Put the Crisco in the skillet along with all of the chicken fat and let it render until you've got the chicken floured and ready to add to the skillet, etc. Put things in the right order so the entire operation goes smoothly. That's the way I put a season together.

As much as you might not like 'administrative' tasks, they are the starting point and they are a necessary part of the job. Establishing the upcoming season's procedures and expectations will pave the way for smooth sailing as you progress into the molding and shaping of your team.

172

The more polished you become in this area, the better relations you will have with the parents. They can make you or break you so you always want them on your side. By anticipating and eliminating the non-playing type of headaches before the season starts, you will position yourself to be able to focus on why you got into this mess in the first place. (That is helping your players put together a successful team.)

When you start working with your players, you can't start with your most complex offensive and defensive schemes. Start with some basics that your players should, but don't necessarily, know. Remember, you might be cleaning up some of the messes created by their previous coaches. Do not assume that because of age, your players know a certain amount.

Probably the most important aspect in teaching players how to compete is to properly develop their attitudes. Start with, "Clean, fair, and legal." I don't care where life's paths take these kids; they need to have that as a basic cornerstone in whatever they choose to do. If you can instill that belief into your players' attitudes, that might be the best favor you ever do for them.

From there, you establish your standards for everything from your players' comportment to their performance in various drills. You may have noticed that I haven't talked specifically about discipline very much. I am a firm believer in discipline on my teams. After all, how can a player develop self-discipline if he doesn't learn discipline with regard to external tasks?

Once you have set your performance standards, there is no compromising them. You must demand that the players conform to your standards, not the other way around. If you slack off or let players slide here and there, you've lost a lot more than just a missed free throw or a missed tackle. You've eroded your credibility in every aspect of your coaching. Trust me on this one because you may not realize it's happening to you until it's too late to reverse the trend.

By taking this approach, you minimize the number of times it becomes necessary to bite the players' heads off. When disciplining players, you can't denigrate or otherwise insult them. You have to address the specific issue(s) that the player needs to improve. You can't insult his intelligence or manliness. Still, if a player has failed, by something within his control, to live up to the standards as they have been established, he needs to hear about it.

I have tossed kids out of practices for various transgressions. Although it always came as a surprise to players, they knew they deserved it. It might have taken some time before they came around to my way of thinking but eventually they did so.

I have developed a reputation as an uncompromising coach where the standards of performance are concerned without being regarded as a chronically negative yeller and screamer. Don't get me wrong; I am not soft on my players. I let them have it when they deserve it, but generally they bring their maximum effort to practice every play every day. That's all I've ever asked and that's all any coach can ask.

I think you can tell from reading this book that my techniques are very successful. I have only included a fraction of examples on how I've gotten my message across over the years. There were undefeated teams in football, basketball, and baseball that I have not included in this book. I could go on *ad nauseum* with stories from all of my teams – and you may think I've already done so – but all of the stories I've shared have had important teaching moments. I think you can get a good feel of how I handle teams from what I've shared.

My players understand that the team is far more important than any given player. Sometimes with male egos, that is a difficult concept to get players to understand. If you look at the best of the best throughout history, they are not the ones who have superior statistics at the expense of their teammates. They may have superior statistics, but they also make other players around them better.

Look at my fullback who didn't carry the ball in the biggest game of the season. He was eager to accept the special challenge of blocking the star defensive player on the other team. Sure, there was a little bit of his male ego involved in competing one on one with that other very talented player, but he knew that for our team to succeed, he had to win the 'game within the game' against Mr. Weatherford. He knew that that contribution was far more important than any yards he might have gained personally.

My running backs were always vicious blockers. Why? They knew that they would not carry the ball if they didn't block for their teammates. It was that simple. By putting it to them that way, it became their decision if they carried the ball or not. When you can put control (sort of) of the team in the hands of the players, they will take pride in making the right things happen. If they are just filling the role that you assigned, their performance will be more mechanical and unimaginative. (Go stand on the block.)

My quarterback who called his own plays never even thought about calling his own number all of the time. (You may have seen teams where the offense was quarterback right, quarterback left, and quarterback up the middle.) With my teams, it was quite the opposite. I had to persuade him to carry the ball. I had to talk to him about how important his physical contribution was to the success of the team. He knew that he was calling almost all of the plays so mentally he was contributing, but we needed his legs too, not just his brains.

Also, think about defending against one running back versus defending against a whole stable of them. I have had the same issue with basketball teams. I wanted all of my players to be capable of scoring. Of course, I would take an excellent defensive player who never scores a point for me any time. The point here is that it is easier to defend a basketball team with one player averaging forty points and the other players scoring five points per game, than it is if each of the five starters averages twelve points per game.

I recently ran into two of my former high school basketball players. They brought up the subject of their performance during their senior season. They both volunteered that they were too arrogant and selfish to put the team first. No, I didn't prompt them to admit that. I was actually surprised, but very pleased, by their admission.

Another coach and I took over their program prior to their senior season. We've already identified how difficult it can be to shape the minds of teenage boys. They already know more than you do; just ask them. Plus, there's always Susie in Chemistry class taking their minds off of what you're trying to teach them.

If we would have started with these seniors and their teammates when they were freshmen, we would have had them clicking on all cylinders by their junior year at the latest. They can look back now and understand the messages we were teaching but our concepts were relatively new to them at the time. Their collective approach to basketball was already etched in stone and not much of it included selfless teamwork.

That goes back to a lineage of coaches who just didn't understand the complete picture of how to develop the right attitude among the ball players. That takes time and it's best to start early. These kids had very good physical talent, but they had received very little coaching above the shoulders. You have the opportunity to address that. Do not gloss over it.

******

I once had the father of one of my former youth football players look me up to tell me about his 8th grade son's first experience in the high school football program. It seems that the eight graders were invited to lift weights at the high school after school. This boy was the only one who went and being rather shy, a little on the smallish side, and still carrying his baby fat, he was a bit intimidated when he got there.

Another of my former players was a senior. He introduced himself to the younger boy and taught him how to use each machine properly. He asked about the player's position and then showed him on which exercises he should concentrate to benefit that position the most. The older boy understood the value of the whole football program so

178

instead of hazing the young kid; he took him under his wing. That meant a lot to the young player and by extension, to his father also.

I have always looked at participation in sports as nothing more than an analogy for life. The percentage of participants that ultimately makes a living playing sports is miniscule. The vast majority of your players are going to go into the, "real world." The sport in which you are coaching them is simply a teaching tool. It is a way that you can help your players get a leg up on the competition as they grow older. Don't lose sight of that fact.

To be successful in whatever endeavors they choose, they will need to know how to compete, "clean, fair, and legal." They need to know how to get the most out of their abilities. To do that, they are going to have to push themselves - and prevail at some things they really don't like - without quitting. They are going to have to accept failure as well as success with equal grace. You will have a lot to do with how they learn this very basic fact of life by how you teach it to your players.

No matter how good my teams were, we never totally destroyed an opponent. Sure, there were some lopsided scores, but in football, we never scored more than the thirty-three points we scored in that one championship game. Our typical scores that season were 26 – 6. We scored enough to be in control, but we never humiliated anybody. In basketball, if we could win by forty, we were content to win by twenty.

There was no need to humiliate another team. You never make your own team any better by running up the score against a lesser opponent. If you feel that you have to resort to that sort of methodology, you are negating many of the good things you have the opportunity to teach your players.

Also, I felt it was more valuable to give our less experienced players as much playing time as possible, rather than to run up the score and amass some gaudy statistics. Remember that I pointed out that I had many more football players who could actually play the game than the other teams in the league? Granted, some of that came from knowing the available players and choosing the more talented ones. But most of it came from giving the lesser players significant playing time along the way, not just the last few meaningless kneel down snaps of lopsided games.

Football takes an awful lot of hard work. (Duh!) I mean, nearly all multiple sport participants will tell you that football is the most grueling. You can't expect all of your players to come out to practice every day with the same piss and vinegar if they don't see any immediate benefit, i. e., playing time. Therefore; the harder my substitutes worked, the more playing time they earned.

Treating players that way will build credibility for your program. Add to that the fact that, in most youth leagues, there is a fee involved and parents expect to see little Johnny on the playing field in part because of that check they wrote at the beginning of the season. I played my substitute players as much as possible in lopsided wins because I knew there might be some games where the score would remain close and the starters would carry the day. To this day, I have never had a parent question why little Johnny didn't get more playing time. (The lone exception was Bobby's dad whom you have read about, but technically I was the assistant so that blemish goes on the head coach's resume. O. k., I'm just kidding – and anyway, we got that situation corrected.)

I frequently see former players out in social settings. The toughest thing is recognizing them. You see, they've grown up since I last saw them. I haven't changed as much. My former high school players are the easiest to recognize because they have changed the least.

It is always embarrassing when I don't recognize a former player right off the bat. I have prepared for situations like these by preparing my sons ahead of time. If one of my sons happens to be with me, and I don't immediately introduce him; that is his clue that I have no idea who this bright-eyed individual is. My son will step forward and introduce himself thereby giving me the opportunity to hear the player's name when he reciprocates the introduction. This has worked – and saved me much embarrassment - on many occasions.

If I am on my own, things are a bit trickier. I have learned the art of humility on occasion when I didn't recognize my player and didn't own up to it immediately. When he asked me a pointed question about a specific instance regarding his playing days with me, I listened very closely for a clue. Sometimes I got nothing. No team name, no other players' names, nothing that even gave me a remote chance to pinpoint who this eager faced young man was. Quick, where is a dark hole for me to crawl in and hide? I have gotten better at admitting my failures.

Now, if I don't know a player immediately, I tell him so right up front. That eliminates the potential for embarrassment right away. I apologize for not remembering his name, and when I learn who the player is, I go into some 'remember when' story that shows the player I really do remember him; I just lost his name momentarily. Hey, I'm getting old so forgetfulness is expected, right? When I can relate a couple of stories from his playing days with me, it makes the player feel appreciated, knowing that I remember his contributions to our team. It's better that the player thinks I'm just old and forgetful than to think that I just didn't remember him at all.

It is always a pleasure seeing my former players because they always have fond memories of playing for me. Again, it's not because I coddled them; it's because they appreciated the discipline, the knowledge, the victories, or the pizza parties. (What player doesn't appreciate a good pizza party?) Sure, they might remind me of some of my less than stellar moments, but still, there are good times to reminisce.

Several of my players routinely vie for the championship of our annual city golf tournament. (I did not coach them in golf, but hopefully, I helped with the mental approach to sports that is such a key in golf.) I have players who have gone on to success in medical school, engineering, financial planning, entrepreneurship, and many other challenging careers. When it's all said and done, seeing what these former players accomplish is as good a reward as you could ask for from your coaching career. Hopefully, the lessons they learned from you helped them along the way.

The End

§